The Beat Interviews

by John Tytell

Published by Beatdom Books

Praise for The Beat Interviews

Tytell is a great companion. Here at the top of his form he celebrates the Beats with his all-encompassing sensitivity to the major writers. Tytell's deep commitment and warm personal insights shine through *The Beat Interviews*.

– Ann Charters, author of *Kerouac: A Biography*, and editor of *Kerouac: Selected Letters 1940-1956.*

Just when we thought there was nothing more to say about the Beat Generation, John Tytell's new book is refreshing. At the heart of the book are his interviews, conducted when the key figures were alive and talking. The straightforward Q and A format allows us to hear their distinctive voices before they were edited and tidied up as literary history. It is rare to be able to enjoy the oral voice so clearly.

– Steven Watson, author of *The Birth of the Beat Generation.*

In addition to being one of the country's leading scholars in the field of Beat Studies, John Tytell was intimate with most of the era's major literary figures. That fact alone makes these interviews indispensable. He has interspersed insightful essays throughout this exceptional collection of interviews, to reveal each writer as a truly unique individual. Nevertheless they somehow merged to form one of America's greatest generations of authors. Tytell's enlightened and unsurpassed approach makes for worthwhile reading and is a researcher's dream.

– Bill Morgan, author of *The Beat Generation in San Francisco: A Literary Guide* and editor of *Howl on Trial: The Battle for Free Expression.*

It is wonderful to start the book with Huncke and so nice to also read and therefore be in the same room with Carl. And the second Chapter The COOL World sets up Holmes interview, and is really important stuff. And all the essays in the book are really well done and INTERESTING!! So if this new book can excite an 83 year old, imagine what a gift this book will be to younger folks!!

– David Amram, author of *Offbeat: Collaborating with Kerouac.*

If John Tytell's new book were merely a re-visit to these stars of the Beat Generation from an earlier time, *The Beat Interviews* would be a valuable reminder of who they were to anyone interested in this unique counter cultural literati. But, this slim volume is so much more. Interwoven with the writers' first hand accounts, Tytell's sharp analysis, honed by decades-long scrutiny, updates the record and corrects the revisionism as time moves farther from the facts. The impulse to mythologize, inherent to the Beat movement, is busted here, and the truth is so much more exciting. Now that the beat writers have entered history, this book is essential reading for understanding their lives and literature, from a critic who was there from the beginning.

– Regina Weinreich, author of *Kerouac's Spontaneous Poetics* and editor of Kerouac's *Book of Haikus.*

For my love, Mellon.

Published by Beatdom Books

Cover photograph © 2014 Mellon Tytell
Photo was taken at Allen Ginsberg's farm in Cherry Valley, New York in 1973. From left to right: Carl Solomon, Allen Ginsberg, Peter Orlovsky, and John Tytell.

View the publisher's website:
www.books.beatdom.com

Printed in the United Kingdom
First Print Edition
ISBN 978-0-9569525-9-2

The Beat Interviews

I Origins

Huncke Interview
p.1

The Cool World
p.20

II Philosophy

John Clellon Holmes Interview
p.29

The Joyous Disease
p.58

III Burroughs

Burroughs Interview
p.66

Hello Mr. Nice Guy
p.90

Call Him Burroughs
p.115

IV "I'm with you in Rockland"

Carl Solomon Interview
p.124

The Comedian As Common Denominator
p.141

V Ginsberg

A Conversation With Allen Ginsberg
p.148

"The Greatest Man in San Francisco"
p.162

Requiem for Ginsberg
p.168

i.
Origins
An Interview with Herbert Huncke

Herbert Huncke was a legend in his own time. Dragging himself "through the negro streets at dawn looking for an angry fix," he was one of the original members of the Beat Generation. A furtive figure who appears several times in "Howl," was celebrated as Herman in Burroughs' *Junkie*, as Elmo Hassel in Jack Kerouac's *On the Road*, and Huck in *Visions of Cody*, Huncke participated in the quest for forbidden experience that brought William Burroughs, Jack Kerouac, and Allen Ginsberg together in New York City just after World War II. Indeed, although he would modestly demur, Huncke introduced them to aspects of life of which they were previously unaware, and which profoundly affected both the content and character of their writing.

The word "beat" was frequently used by Huncke to signify exhaustion. In an exposed, defeated, vagrant state, one beyond humiliation, he could afford to be confessional because there was nothing further to lose. Huncke was so beaten down to his "naked human core," as Allen Ginsberg once put it, that he was on the radiant edge of illumination. What may have seemed new and dangerous to Burroughs, Kerouac, and Ginsberg came almost naturally to Huncke. Hitchhiking around America, shipping out on freighters, the Times Square hustle and the hipster scene constituted his education, yet he had an authentic lore to share. Much of his special knowledge was expressed in his lifestyle; an affront to middle-class expectations, he has been a source of inspiration to other writers. Like Rimbaud, he has taught that consciousness can be extended through *dereglement des sens*, (violent derangement of the senses) and he has experimented with many drugs. In one week in the winter of 1945, he introduced Burroughs, Ginsberg, and Kerouac to morphine and redirected the course of American letters.

Although his intention has never been grander than surviving on a daily basis, he has affected our changing culture in many subtle ways, not the least of which was his series of meetings with Dr. Alfred Kinsey in New York City. Huncke's vision has been shaped by forces – prison, the drug underworld – that many contemporary writers have sought to simulate because of the terrifying honesty often found there. A pariah figure, he was drawn into the early Beat circle in the apartment they shared at 419 West 115th Street in 1945 because he offered entry to a new subject matter, the underground hipster scene, but also because of his abilities as a *raconteur*. In addition to a remarkable capacity for reciprocity and an unusual tolerance of differences, what made this group cohere was the interest they expressed in each other's stories. His first book, *Huncke's Journals*, was published by The Poets Press in 1965 in New York. Subsequently, his stories have appeared in *The Evening Sun Turned Crimson* (Cherry Valley Editions, 1980) followed by an autobiography, *Guilty Of Everything* (Paragon Press, 1990).

This interview took place on March 2, 1973, through the generous hospitality of Rlene Dahlberg; also convivially present were David Sands and Kevin O'Connell.

***

John Tytell: I wanted to ask about your friendship with the other Beat writers, Ginsberg, Kerouac and Burroughs.

Herbert Huncke: I've known Ginsberg since he was about nineteen as a young man in college. I met him at the same time that I met Kerouac, Bill Burroughs, and a very interesting woman that lived with Bill Burroughs, Joan Adams. There were a number of others. I met them all at the same time.

JT: Was that in the early forties?

HH: Yes, I think around the latter part of '43 and '44. No, no, no. I can pin it better than that. The end of 1945 because I met Burroughs first. I had been going to sea at the time with a fellow named Phil White. Later on Burroughs became very interested in him, and they became good friends. What had happened was this: I had gone to sea with Phil ostensibly to kick a habit, that was the main reason. We went aboard a tanker. Phil was a messman and I was a second-cook. We grabbed what was known as a hot ship, it was just the tail end of the war and it was a six month trip. I found it very interesting, acquired a pet monkey at the time, stayed very high, came back, and a fellow that I knew, Bob Brandenberg had met Burroughs. He was out of Cleveland, he and his brother Don, and they had a big thing about being gangsters, and it was Bob's desire to be a mobster of some kind, and as a result he had a very fast-going patter about the underworld. He had gotten a job working as a soda jerk in a drugstore not far from Columbia University, and while he was working behind the counter, every other afternoon or so, Burroughs had the habit of coming into the drugstore and sitting down at the counter. Apparently he did live in the neighborhood. He was taking some kind of course at Columbia. He got to rapping with Bob and Bob gave him a little bit of a come on, and one day Burroughs leaned across the counter and asked Bob if he knew where he could get rid of a sawed-off shotgun and several boxes of morphine syrettes. Bob immediately thought of me, and knew that I was just about due back, and also was quite interested in Burroughs himself. This guy really startled him. Bob suggested that Burroughs come downtown to this pad on Henry Street on the Lower East Side which was a kind of a hangout for thieves and all sorts of people.

JT: Was Bill Gaines there?

HH: No, I met him originally, and introduced him to Burroughs, and I met him in jail. He was an interesting guy but Gaines wasn't his last name, I'm trying to think of it, turned out he was the son of a banker somewhere in Ohio who had been disowned, and was paid to stay away – he received a bit of money every month from his father. He also was a very strange man. He was well along in years when I met him. I had been sentenced to doing six months in jail. At that time Rikers Island was set up considerably different than it is now, and for certain types of convictions they had huge dormitories out in the main building, and these dormitories held about fifty men sleeping in beds lined up in rows. I was assigned to a bed as soon as I arrived, and as I was putting my things away in a locker next to the bed and sort of casing the place, looking the scene over, I became aware of this guy in the next bed who was a tall thin gaunt looking man, almost bald but graying, very loose features, long dangling arms, sunken eyes, and a very elegant way of speaking. Later I introduced him to Burroughs.

JT: What was your life like at that time?

HH: I had just come from 42nd St. as a hustler in about my third year. I had hit New York when I was about seventeen, once very briefly for a short stay before this period and stayed about two months. I got involved in a very strange series of happenings. I had hitchhiked from Chicago.

JT: In your journals you mention that you are from Chicago.

HH: Basically, I was raised there but am actually from Greenfield, Massachusetts. Anyway, that's what I was doing, living on 42nd St.

JT: Had you started shipping out at this time?

HH: No, that began at the tail-end of that period. Going to sea had always been a dream of mine like joining the circus when I was a kid.

JT: Did you ever belong to a circus?

HH: No, but I like circus people. Well, I like freak show people. I've met real circus people but I've never been intimate with them, I've known several tattoo people that worked sideshows, and one half man half woman person, Elsie-John, that's my story "Elsie."[1]

JT: When did you go down to Texas with Bill and Joan Burroughs?

HH: The Spring of 1947. I was there from February until the first week of October.

JT: Where was that in Texas?

---

1 "Elsie John" was Huncke's first attempt at a short story, and was published in 1979.

HH: That was in a place called New Waverly, which was in East Texas, out of Houston about fifty miles over a paved highway, and then this little town on either side of the highway, and you would turn off the highway and hit a macadam road that led back into pine woods and bayou country, very beautiful low rolling country with little weather beaten farmhouses owned by black people, then over an old dirt road for about two miles into the pine woods.

JT: Were Cassady and Ginsberg and Kerouac there at that time?

HH: No they weren't there. Kerouac, to my knowledge, never was there. Ginsberg and Cassady visited there.

JT: Wasn't that the time that you were helping them build a bed?

HH: That's a funny story. I felt sort of guilty about it for no reason whatsoever. Let me explain the situation. Ginsberg, who was a young man at that time, curly haired, and starry eyed, a dreamer and in love with life, very sad at the same time, a typical young poet is what he was, he also considered becoming a teacher, he probably would have been a good one, he was also interested in history. He liked me or maybe I held a sort of evil influence over him, let's put it that way, I don't know, I've often wondered how he feels about that. I don't feel that way but he might. Anyway, he and Neal were on their way down from San Francisco to visit us in Texas, and I had met Neal briefly in New York and heard stories about him and knew that Allen was very interested in him, they were good companions, lovers, I suppose, not that anyone paid much attention to that. Knowing that they were coming I thought it might be a good idea to give up my room to them, and I liked sleeping on a screened in porch we had where I could lie at night and hear armadillos, and see the moon through Spanish moss draped trees, and strange night sounds, the forest all around, like a paradise really. You have to see it: little old weather beaten cabin, silver grey. It consisted originally of two gigantic rooms cut into four with a low porch in front. I had a very good room off to one side, I had puttered around with it and made it quite comfortable, so I thought they would probably want to be together; why not give them my room? Now, one of the things I had never been able to satisfy was my bed situation. I had a cot with a mattress on it but I had never really liked it. I didn't know what to do about a bed situation for the two of them. I wasn't thinking of them going to bed together but....

JT: Just as a place to sleep?

HH: Right. Anyway, there were several pieces of board around. At one time Burroughs' people had sent down some beds from St. Louis and one of them had never been used. So I conceived of getting these sideboards together in some kind of a bed situation. The only place to work was dead in front of the cabin so it was a whole thing, everybody could see me busy with that fucking bed.

JT: And you were trying to nail it together?

HH: Solid. And I did work on it because I figured that I had a practical idea. Unfortunately while I was working on it, they arrived, Burroughs was busy in his usual fashion shuffling around and playing the landed gentry, I guess. He'd go out with his pistol and do a lot of shooting at the side of the barn, target practice. It used to sound off through the woods, a couple of people asked if there were gangsters living over there.

JT: Did you do any hunting then?

HH: No, just target practice. What are you going to hunt? Once he shot an armadillo and it was such an unpleasant thing. I suggested it, I'm ashamed of myself for having done it. Afterwards I buried it and said prayers over it.

JT: Was there a sense of community among the group?

HH: You mean a formal community? No. They may have thought so but I didn't. Do you want to hear my interest in the group? I started out wanting to be a writer as a young boy among other things; at one time I intensely wanted to be a dancer. I wanted to be an actor and I wanted to write and travel all over the world, and I started being very active even in Chicago. My family background was sort of strange, it was middle-class and bourgeois except that my mother and father were divorced. I don't want to go into a whole story but it was a typical scene. One thing about it is that I broke away from the family as often and as quickly as possible; I just didn't want to be involved. I fought furiously and angrily with my mother all the time, we screamed at each other, I'd really go out of my mind.

JT: How old were you when you left?

HH: The first time? Well, intentionally, the first time I ran away from home I was about six years old, but I chickened out. I started splitting from home when I was twelve.

Rlene Dahlberg: When did you leave finally and never go back?

HH: Go back to what? There was no home to go back to. My mother was a beautiful woman, a stunning woman, but she should never have had children.

RD: Well how old was she when she got married?

HH: Fifteen.

RD: Well, that tells the story.

HH: And in a funny way too because she was a small town Western girl who didn't know her ass from her elbow and nobody had ever explained, she probably caught sound of things but sex was a dirty word. It was a certain nasty hangover from the Victorian thing.

JT: So then you came to New York?

HH: I had gone around the country a couple of times before I came to New York to stay in the last months of 1939.

JT: Was there a time when you were living on the Lower East Side when you saw a lot of Burroughs, on Henry Street?

HH: These questions are so loaded! They all are the result of so many other things happening. All right: Henry Street. I knew nothing about the Lower East Side except what I had seen in movies. I had gotten my start – how else was I going to – on 42nd Street. I couldn't work; I didn't know how to work really. I didn't work in New York for a long time. I just started hustling, just knocking around, you know, scrounging, learning I guess. If anybody would have told me as a kid that I'd ever get to know honest to god thieves or ever be in a place where there was a gun...

JT: Was that like a hipster scene?

HH: We didn't think of it that way. I certainly knew that what was going down was hip, yeah, I knew the word hip, hipster, all of those words, that's old jazz musician talk that goes back to the thirties when they used to have in jazz what was called jam sessions. Jazz musicians would get together and play their kind of music. Of course Chicago has always been a big music city, and there was a whole black section that was just loaded with black and white musicians and a little junk, a lot of pot, marijuana, tea we called it.

RD: The near North Side was where that happened, wasn't it?

HH: I tell you what made up the near North Side: dikes, faggots, a certain so-called hip element, the swish places and the chi-chi places, the Drake, the Coq D'Or, there were several bars, the K-9, the first jazz joints, the Blue Note, I guess, the Three Deuces, but I'm talking about places in the black section on the South Side of Chicago, the Harlem section, Cottage Grove, South State Street, the El Dorado, places like that where they used to put on a great show, you know, you'd be about three sheets to the wind in a place just packed with people, sitting at the table, all juicing, and a really wild band beating out frantic jazz and maybe a platform built like a boxing ring dead in the center of the place.

JT: What year was this?

HH: The early thirties. You'd go up there and dance, just stand up there and rub against each other in time to music, it was kind of wild, then you'd intermittently rest while these black chicks would come out and really put on a show, and there would always be a headliner, a Billie Holliday type scene, the big jazz mommas. Now how did I get started on that?

JT: We were talking about hipsters.

HH: That's right. Anybody that knew those people or moved with them could be affected. For example, there was a place called the El Dorado, they had on Sunday morning what was known as a breakfast dance. All the musicians that played the nightclubs around town would knock off at four or five in the morning. At six they would hit the El Dorado, plus people who had been partying all night long, you'd go in there, doors would be shut, smoke a little bit, and a band would play, they'd work out sounds and everybody would sit around and be mellow. Then you'd drive out to the sand dunes in Indiana, stay stoned, shoot up a little junk maybe, little cocaine, joy-pop.

JT: That's quite a combo.

HH: Then go swimming. Those were the days. That's how the so called hip-jive started, and it became part of the scene. Like the word beat, I think really indirectly Allen should take credit for the word beat, although I used the word all the time but I never meant it in a beatific sense.

JT: You meant down? The city against you?

HH: I meant beaten. The world against me.

JT: But everybody used the word?

HH: Well, in a beatific way, oddly enough. I'm sure, if you were a soul brother, you were a soul brother. I don't think I ever used that term but it explains it.

JT: Everybody seemed to have been experimenting with drugs at that time – Burroughs, Ginsberg, and Kerouac?

HH: That's a good question. I guess so, they shared that interest. Even before I met Burroughs he had an interest in drugs. We met as a result of drugs. I had only known him a short while, and I knew that he was living in an apartment not far from Columbia University, on 115th Street, the Morningside Drive area. The apartment was really owned by Joan Adams who was a young woman whose family lived in Tuxedo Park. She was taking a course in journalism at Columbia. She had already – I hate to say for sure but I think she had gone to Barnard at one time. When I met her she was part of a so-called college intellectual crowd which consisted of Burroughs, Ginsberg, Kerouac. Her old man Adams I had never met but she'd been making the scene with Adams who was a writer too, a young ardent student type – what their relationship had been I don't know but he got her pregnant and she had her child, a very beautiful little girl named Julie who clung to her mother and imitated her mother's mannerisms. Wherever Joan was Julie was there too.

JT: Joan was supposed to have been a very striking woman?

HH: Oh boy! I don't know how to describe her. I've never met a woman like Joan. I don't know how to explain her. I think I fell sort of in love with her in a funny way. At one time I think she loved me in return. I think toward the end though I had done something that turned her against me – she had very decided likes and dislikes – and I think I did something to cause her to lose respect for me but just what I don't know for sure. At any rate she was very much in love with Burroughs in a strange way. They did not have an ardent sex life at all, as you know Burroughs is decidedly homosexual in his interests. I was amazed to discover that he had been physical with Joan. I had never suspected that he might be, but apparently he was because his son is very much his son, there's no question about that.

JT: His son is a writer too?

HH: Yes, he's become one. The relationship between father and son is very strange, I gather. I have never met his son although I was in Texas when his son was born. Joan was pregnant during that time in 1947, and three o'clock one morning I heard them sort of moving around, and Joan had knocked on Bill's door to announce that she had better go to the hospital, it was about time for her to have her baby. They got out and climbed into the jeep and drove out into the night. They hadn't made any kind of arrangements at all, but there was a local hospital and she went and had her baby, and the next day she was back again with the baby.

JT: Did they go to Mexico after that?

HH: Yes, their trip to Mexico happened the following year, and at that time I was not seeing them at all.

JT: Where did you go after that?

HH: I came back to New York, we all did.

JT: Cassady as well?

HH: Oh yes, Cassady as well. Ginsberg came back – I'll venture to say – by train. Joan and Julie got back by train.

But Cassady, Burroughs, and myself drove back in the jeep with the whole back of the jeep packed with mason jars full of pot.

JT: That you had grown?

HH: Yes, the whole works.

JT: That's a long drive?

HH: I didn't do any driving. Cassady did.

JT: Was Cassady that good a driver, "greatest driver" as he's known?

HH: Cassady could drive a car, let me tell you.

JT: Did he drive at high speeds?

HH: If he wanted to. He wasn't a frantic driver by any means. He was a good driver, some people feel a car and they know how to handle it. He knew pretty much what a car would do. I always felt comfortable with him driving.

JT: Cassady made this supposedly amazing impression on people. Did you feel that?

HH: Oh yes. First of all he was an extremely handsome physical looking cat to both men and women. He was really good-looking which he never lost even as he grew older, except it coarsened a little bit. He came out looking like a certain type of prisoner. Once in a while you'll see a man who comes out of jail after serving a long period of time who fits into the category I'm speaking about.

JT: Was his primary drug speed?

HH: He was into everything a lot, except junk. He might have tried heroin, but speed was his kick, amphetamine.

JT: Was it a pretty constant thing?

HH: Yes it was.

JT: Was that what was making his life move so quickly?

HH: Well, that's a tough one to answer. If that was the only thing that was making his life move, no, it was part of it. He had a great deal of energy and drive and interest of his own.

JT: Did you see him during the time that he was driving for Kesey's Merry Pranksters?[2]

HH: Yes, I met Kesey then. It was when their bus had just pulled into New York. They had moved into a big apartment up on Madison Avenue, a great big plush apartment, and they were sort of camping in there, a whole crowd, with this big bus down in front of the building that had been painted in psychedelic colors. They had traveled clear across the country with this, with tape recorders and cameras, and beautiful girls. Oh god you should have seen some of those chicks. Every cat had a chick, there was probably about ten couples all together, maybe more. And Cassady driving the bus.

JT: Supposedly at very high speeds around curves with an instinct about what was ahead on the road.

HH: He was all right. He was never reckless, he wasn't a reckless driver.

JT: And he wasn't a reckless person?

HH: Not really. He had a devil may care attitude, of course. And even that was curbed. He was a very nervous, worried cat all the time. He died in Mexico, you know, on a railroad track incidentally, staggered out in the night balls ass naked, supposedly out of his head on goof balls. He wanted to die all the time anyway. He could never find a chick to settle with. He made it with lots of chicks, he was a very sexy guy, married several times and having affairs with cats too. He had a very violent love affair with Ginsberg, I

2 Ken Kesey (1935-2001), author of *One Flew Over the Cuckoo's Nest*, and founder of the Merry Pranksters. Considered an intermediary between the Beats and hippies.

mean it was very active both sexually and mentally.

JT: Did they ever live together?

HH: Not just like that, no. They were in each other's company for periods of time. The Denver scene I don't know much about except what I've heard.

JT: When did you meet Dr. Kinsey?[3]

HH: When he first came to New York to do his research, I think after the war. I'm trying to remember the year, and I'm also trying to recall whether I had met Kinsey before I had met Burroughs, but I think I met Burroughs first, because they were together at one point, I had introduced them. In fact, we used to make up a table in a bar, there would be Kinsey, Burroughs, Kerouac, Kerouac's wife Edie, myself, sometimes Joan, plus stray characters and others who would float in and out, at a bar called The Angler. We'd meet in the evening, and Burroughs would usually spring for a dinner or drinks for everybody, or he'd be looking to cop pot, and I'd make the connection for him. Of course Kinsey was doing interviews, and he would pay for them. I used to get people from 42nd Street for him. That's how I met him. He had observed me on the scene and sent a young student to approach me in a cafeteria. I couldn't believe that he just wanted to hear about my sex life. I guess I was one of his first subjects.

JT: Did you meet with Kinsey frequently?

HH: Many times. Also at that time, Bill Gaines, whose real last name I can't remember,[4] used to come, he was living in a little room on 44th Street at the time, just off Eighth Avenue. He and Ginsberg became very friendly for a while, Ginsberg found him an interesting person. Gaines used to steal overcoats, he had a hustle where he'd go in a

3 Alfred Kinsey (1894-1956), founder of the Institute for Sex Research and author of the *Kinsey Reports*.

4 His real name was William Garner; Bill Gaines was the name given to him by Jack Kerouac in his novels.

restaurant where coats would be hanging up, and at that time you could sell an overcoat for maybe five dollars, seven dollars. He would get up a few of them during the course of a day. He also helped a few people. I think Ginsberg's brother once bought a coat from him, I think he gave one to Allen once.

JT: But he influenced Burroughs mostly?

HH: Yes. Burroughs and Kerouac write about Gaines living in Mexico just before Burroughs shot Joan, I guess, I don't know too much about that period of time. While that was going on I was in prison, by the way. In fact, the FBI came up to visit me while I was in prison. I was called out one day to the front of the administration building and there were two government agents, I guess they were FBI, and they had some photostatic copies of letters that I had written, that Burroughs had written, that Ginsberg had written, mail that Burroughs had received while in New Orleans. You know I was so green at the time that when they called me in and started reading these letters to me, it never occurred to me that since they were my letters I couldn't see them and I started to reach for them and man this guy said "Oh no!" And Burroughs had opened up, and I had told him about a ride in a stolen car I had taken.

JT: Jane Kramer tells about this ride in a stolen car that you took with Allen.[5]

HH: She's the first person that ever tried to tell that story.

RD: The Utopia Parkway ride.

HH: Is that what she calls it? It was that, incidentally, that ended disastrously, where a kid called Jack Melody and his old lady were driving a car with Ginsberg sitting in the back clutching his school books with all sorts of notations in them, and addresses and so on. Meanwhile, all of us had been living together in an apartment on York Avenue

5 Jane Kramer is the author of *Allen Ginsberg in America.*

up in the seventies which had originally belonged to Ginsberg, but now we were all living there, all using junk, except Allen, periodically he'd taste a little bit. One thing I admire about Allen is that he has always had the strength of his convictions. He samples what he preaches. He has his own way of handling the situation but he likes to turn on, thoroughly enjoys it, he doesn't make any issue out of it at all. He's tried almost every drug I can think of. Also he has a certain openness that's always made me love him. He has narrow conceptions at times too but usually he's very open.

JT: Do drugs enhance that openness?

HH: I don't know. I was on the David Susskind Show and he asked me questions like that. If I say yes then I'm in the position of justifying the thing which isn't necessarily true. Neither am I denying it. I think it's helped me a little bit. I've done some good things under amphetamine. My automatic writing, that was a beautiful experience in any language.

JT: Much of your journals were written while using drugs?

HH: I have written under some very strange circumstances, most of my writing has always been under strange conditions. I sometimes don't think I'm much of a writer, but I write, or put it down on paper, or have, I'm not doing that much anymore.

JT: Ginsberg dedicated his *Empty Mirror* to you for *The Confessions*. Had he been reading them?

HH: He's always had access to what I've done. He hasn't read all I've written. Whatever was around when I was near him, I've read it to him. I was doing a little writing consistently, not exactly on schedule. He's always been very encouraging as far as writing was concerned. You asked me a question a long time ago about what we had in the way of interests in each other, and I started to tell you what I thought I had, or my interests, or the appeal these people had for me. They were all creative people, and I started telling you that I wanted to be a dancer, and then an actor, and a writer. But I always respected people who did something in the way of creative endeavor, so to speak. I didn't know anything, but I was interested, so I felt a certain kinship. I wanted them all to be writers, and I felt attracted by their potential, and encouraged it as often as possible.

JT: Did you know Kerouac as well as the others?

HH: I was more interested in Ginsberg and Burroughs. Kerouac was on the scene but we weren't nearly as intimate as I was with the others. I saw him but not as often, nor in as friendly circumstances.

JT: Did you think of him as a writer?

HH: No, I didn't. It never occurred to me that he would ever write.

JT: And you appear in several of his novels, including *On the Road* and *Visions of Cody*?

HH: Sure. I was very pleased, duly flattered that I was part of that scene. I was very amused to find myself part of that crowd.

JT: The Beats seem to be really coming into their own now as a movement?

HH: About movements, I don't know. What's a movement?

JT: A few people who say something in a similar way and live in a similar way?

HH: I'll tell you, from the standpoint of what's been done for literature. You know all those people sort of jacked up an interest in literature and poetry, something that had been sorely lacking. I guess there's always been such a group. Bohemians, is that what they're called? Well, you're interested in those things, aren't you? Everybody here is.

The COOL World

The press release accompanying my copy of *The Cool School* (Library of America, 2013) begins by assuring me that "From music, to television, to fashion, hipsters are everywhere today." Actually, with the mordant wit he often displayed, the former *New York Times* book reviewer Anatole Broyard once argued that the hipster's state of mind was inevitably *nowhere*. He might have added that the television screen is the last place one should expect to find anything hip.

Glenn O'Brien's useful anthology - he playfully calls it his "compendium of orphans" - provides enough examples to illustrate the paradoxical metaphysics of nowhere. In a pithy but insightful introduction, he establishes his *terroir*, and defines the geography of the place he is exploring:

> To be hip is to belong to an underground, a subculture or counterculture, an elective tribe located within a larger community, outsiders inside. It is detached from the main thing and proud of its detachment.

A street person, a spiritual outlaw, an outcast, heretic, or pariah figure, the hipster uses language as part of a disguise reflecting an alternate set of values. Like a Gnostic among the early Christians, that language is often coded, multilayered, swiftly mutating, and often deliberately ambiguous. The hipsters kept talking, as Jack Kerouac once maintained in *Playboy Magazine* (of all places!) in 1959, about "personal experience and vision, nightlong confessions full of hope that had become illicit and repressed by War, stirrings, rumblings of a new soul [until] Huncke appeared to us and said 'I'm beat' with radiant light shining out of his despairing eyes…."

When Herbert Huncke, in the winter of 1945, introduced Burroughs, Kerouac, and Ginsberg to morphine via "the mainline," i.e. injected in the veins above the wrist, he was accomplishing a revolution in the sensibility of American writers. Gertrude Stein may have changed direction and moved to Paris to write after she inhaled the nitrous oxide provided by William James at Harvard at the start of the twentieth century, but Huncke's introduction was even more profound and penetrating, a ritual communion of transgression.

The word "beat" was frequently used by Huncke, a furtive Times Square hustler and petty thief with stories about his circus experiences, who became a code figure for the Beats, an emanation of a subterranean underground world and a street sensibility they admired. For Huncke, "beat" did not signify confused values or loss as Stein had characterized Hemingway's generation; it signified exhaustion and being crushed by the weight of the world, all the blather of being flattened out by the hard knocks of negative experiences leaving one too impoverished to find money for food or housing. In that exposed, broken state, an individual could afford to be extremely open and candid because there was nothing left to lose. Status didn't matter and shame was not a possibility because one could not descend any further, and the emptied out state might allow one to be more receptive to vision. As Allen Ginsberg later explained in a letter to his aunt Hannah Litzky in June of 1958, Huncke's being "beat down to his naked human core" could result in a kind of religious illumination.

The term was popularized by novelist John Clellon Holmes in an article, "This is a Beat Generation" that was published in The *New York Times Magazine* in November of 1952. Holmes had heard Kerouac use the term to describe a painter named Iris Brody, "a ragged skeletal but illuminated junky girl we knew," as Ginsberg put it.

Kerouac and Holmes had been walking in the East Village and Kerouac casually commented that Brody did not represent any vestige of the lost generation, but something new – a "beat generation." In his article, Holmes argued that the "nakedness of mind and soul" that created the beat state was a result of being "pushed up against the wall of oneself," in other words existing without hope or resources, not disillusioned like the writers of the 1920s, not suffering from any loss of faith but certain of the need for it. Despite being beaten down or perhaps in some strange way because of it, they still had a will to believe in a spiritual path.

Kerouac extended the meaning of beat to beatitude in his *Playboy* piece in June of 1959. Kerouac's Catholic childhood and his explorations of Buddhism as a means of weathering his own disappointments when his novel *On the Road* was not published when he wrote it in the early 1950s certainly helped to further such a perspective, one that he later popularized in a novel called *The Dharma Bums.*

His emphasis on beatitude was repeated in interviews and on television, most notoriously when he remarked on the John Wingate television show that he was "waiting for

God to show me his face." On one level, he may have been attempting to correct some of the condescensions of mass media, particularly the caricatures of the Beats in a 1959 *Life* article by Paul O'Neill that displayed an apartment with a potbelly stove, an unfinished poem in a typewriter, bean cans, and a baby playing with beer bottles on the floor. The negative stereotype of the Beats as unwashed, unmotivated, uneducated delinquents who scribbled whatever came to mind, was compounded by the San Francisco gossip columnist Herb Caen after the Soviets successfully launched their Sputnik satellite. Derisively, he called the young people who were reading Kerouac beatniks, and the name became a sticky label with a subversive connotation.

Kerouac articulated what he meant in a piece called "Aftermath: The Philosophy of the Beat Generation." The group he envisaged was formulated because of a "special spirituality":

> A vision of crazy illuminated hipsters suddenly rising and roaming America, serious, curious, bumming and hitchhiking everywhere, ragged, beatific, beautiful in a graceful new way — a vision gleaned from the way we had heard the word *beat* spoken on street corners on Times Square and in the Village, in other cities in downtown-city-night of postwar America — *beat,* meaning down and out but full of intense conviction. We'd even heard old 1910 Daddy Hipsters of the streets speak the word that way, with a melancholy sneer. It never meant juvenile delinquents; it meant characters of special spirituality who didn't gang up but were solitary Bartlebies staring out the dead wall window of our civilization.

The "solitary Bartlebies" to whom Kerouac refers would become the descendants of Melville's absurd protagonist.

Bartleby is a scrivener or clerk who refuses – on the singularly subjective grounds that "I prefer not to" – the quite conventional demands of the indulgent Wall Street attorney who employs him to copy legal documents. Bartleby is the fictional cousin of Henry David Thoreau who was incarcerated in Concord, Massachusetts when he refused to pay a poll tax when he wanted to vote, and wrote "On the Duty of Civil Disobedience" in his jail cell. The message of antinomian resistance of that essay would travel a century later as far as Mahatma Gandhi in India and Martin Luther King. Bartleby ends up incarcerated, curled in the fetal position in Melville's story, withdrawn from the world of getting and spending, and staring at a wall – the "dead wall window of our civilization" in Kerouac's formulation. Bartleby's despair is one of the beginning points of the Beat recognition.

The hipsters, with their protective veil of detachment, saw themselves immediately after World War Two as "cool," a relative, provisional quality that like grace could not be faked, but through what Glenn O'Brien in *The Cool School* calls the "swirling total immersion" culture of the late 1960s became an attitude that spread internationally. O'Brien might have done well to have included a section from Amiri Baraka's *Blues People* where he defines cool as the ability "to be calm, even unimpressed by whatever horror the world might daily propose." Baraka's context is a century of segregation and cool was the mask of equanimity assumed by a saxophonist like Lester Young, wearing shades on stage instead of a Sammy Davis grin.

In its heyday hip became a reactive model for the embalming conformities and insecurities that the early Beats felt in the 1950s. Historians tend to emphasize the ways in which Cold War hysteria was manufactured, a construct to enable the military-industrial complex and guarantee prosperity. The "Take-Cover!" nuclear drills, the pervasive terrors of the Red Scare, the creepy insinuations of McCarthyism and the poisonous untruths sounded in the ears of H.U.A.C., all led to the purges in government, in Hollywood, in the universities, and even in the civil service. The 1950s were also a decade in which the Warren Court ended American *apartheid* with the Brown vs. Board of Education decision in 1954, and then a few years later sanctioned *Tropic of Cancer.* In New York City, a D.J. named Allen Freed with a rhythm and blues format, started playing Little Richard, Chuck Berry, Bo Diddley, and finally Elvis. Lawrence Ferlinghetti created a new vitality for the alternative press scene with City Lights and its publication of *Howl* in 1956. A year earlier, Norman Mailer had published his seminal essay, "The White Negro," in a new magazine called *Dissent*, a name that signified the antinomian discontents that would help to redefine national priorities.

Of course, there was very little that could be considered "cool" about any of this, and Kerouac in his *Playboy* piece coyly suggested that most of his Beat writer pals "belonged to the hot school, naturally since that hard gemlike flame needs a little heat." O'Brien includes Mailer's essay as well as Kerouac's "The Origins of the Beat Generation" (the *Playboy* article) and these two selections along with Anatole Broyard's "Portrait of the Hipster" form the emotional core of his anthology.

Some of O'Brien's selections like the ones from jazz musicians Miles Davis, Art Pepper, or an interview with Kerouac's hero Lester Young, help us to understand the dark corners, the sometimes elliptical or private concerns of the hip or cool cosmos. O'Brien gives us short vignettes by Beat code figures like Huncke describing the openness of a Times Square "pad" right after the end of World War Two, sort of a Beat salon with white furniture and Persian blue walls, and Carl Solomon's "A Diabolist," a five hundred word composition against *ennui* probing the relationship between perversity and a new reality, the surrealist desire to "turn things around to make the ugly beautiful."

O'Brien reprints poems by Gregory Corso and Bob Kaufman, Diane Di Prima's recollection of first discovering "Howl," (though her warm memory of sharing a bath with Ginsberg and Kerouac might have provided a better illustration) and Ed Sanders' "Group-Grope" description of neo-beats merging fornication with poetry on the Lower East Side, circa 1961. Along with essayist Seymour Krim's "Making It," his inciting description of an age when the "address book replaces the soul," such selections do a lot to capture the desperate and animating energies of the moment. Some of O'Brien's choices in the final third of his book, attempts to find contemporary illustrations of hardboiled hip like "Beatnik Executives," his own gentle parody of "Howl," fall flat.

The limitation of O'Brien's collection is that it depends on excerpts which as O'Brien admits can only assemble a sampling, a taste of hip diffidence here or a flash of apocalyptic rage as in the Burroughs selection from *Nova Express.* While tasting has its place in any critical methodology, it is often not lasting or substantial enough for us to remember the flavor. The difference between a taste and a full meal is more than volume or duration and defines the quality of the experience. The advantage of any anthology, however, is that it can highlight salient issues which prove central. This requires some discrimination in the selection process, and a perfect example of O'Brien's success in this sphere is the ten-page clip he takes from Joyce Johnson's *Minor Characters* where Walter Pater's gemlike flame really glows.

Johnson observes that after the publication of *On the Road,* Kerouac noted a "cool that was colder and deader than any hipster's earned fatalism." Kerouac had been the first to exclaim that the Beat mood had died in 1952, probably as soon as Holmes announced it to the world in his *The New York Times* article. So most of the literature we regard as Beat results from the attempt to recapture or memorialize a mood or an attitude that had already changed, perhaps even disappeared.

The problem of using hip as a handle, an organizing principle for an anthology, is that the Beats and the counterculture they helped create were much more polymath, nurtured also by such uncool passions as Buddhism or the political awareness that caused Ginsberg to sit on the railroad tracks near the Rocky Flats nuclear production center in Colorado to block a train carrying plutonium. Active protest is never hip or cool which teaches one to use subterfuge to avoid authority. I knew Carl Solomon pretty well for a few decades and I would submit there was absolutely nothing about him that one could characterize as either hip or cool. Huncke, of course, was another matter.

Cool dies when it becomes a fashion adjective. If your blue suede shoes seem cool today, tomorrow they will get smudged. To the extent that hip could become a commodity, sold as a style in the 1970s as merchandisers could caricature, imitate, and package, it began to vitiate as a cultural force. O'Brien cheerfully admits that he was introduced to this subculture as a twelve year old by television, watching Maynard G. Krebs in T*he Many Loves of Dobie Gillis*. The degradation of hip begins with such cartoon parody and is sustained by a magazine culture and the ad agencies that control it that tried to situate hip as glamorous or somehow appealing so Ginsberg and Kerouac end up wearing Chinos in a Gap advertisement. At the still center of hip is an existential anguish that is ignored in such depictions.

I always saw the lines of that anguish in Herbert Huncke's face. Slouching on the criminal edge, a haunting figure with the darkest circles around his eyes and a ravaged look, the "doomy charisma" the novelist Jonathan Lethem described in a *New Yorker* "Talk of the Town" piece, Huncke was always the hip center of the Beat circle, perhaps because he had less ambition to be recognized than any of the others. When I first tried to talk to him in the early 1970s, he seemed unreachably evasive. As Mailer put it in the beginning of "The White Negro," "You can't interview a hipster because his main goal is to keep out of a society which, he thinks, is trying to make everyone over in its own image." When a friend finally set up a meeting at the widow of writer Edward Dahlberg's apartment, Huncke was wound up in a grimace and tight as a cork in a bottle of wine. I understood that he suspected anyone who wanted to ask questions, that previously he had only been interviewed (or should we say "intimidated?") by detectives at Riker's Island, and that what he knew could compromise his freedom and the safety of others. I think he only relaxed and began to trust in me when I lit a joint of *sensimillia* and passed it to him. He knew that a cop might try to set him up, but probably wouldn't have cheerfully inhaled, certainly nothing as strong as what I was proffering. Huncke was gracious to me on that occasion and for the next few decades, and nothing could be cooler than that.

ii.
Philosophy

An Interview with John Clellon Holmes

For over twenty years, John Clellon Holmes and Jack Kerouac shared a special friendship. It began as a literary friendship: Kerouac showing Holmes the journal entries and notebook drafts of a novel that he was arduously composing into his first published book, *The Town and The City*; Holmes eager to learn about the new world which Kerouac inhabited, and its strangely illuminated orbits – Allen Ginsberg, Neal Cassady, Herbert Huncke, Bill Cannastra, and others. Holmes yearned to capture some of the freedom from more traditional allegiances that these figures had won in their respective ways, but for Kerouac he was a bedrock of value, a man whose judgment was dependable because he retained a sure sense of rightness despite an exceptionally volatile environment. Kerouac confided in Holmes because Holmes, too, was ready to abandon the old answers that would no longer work, but even more because Holmes was a serious spirit, a man genuinely struggling in his art and in his life to discover valid responses in an anxious time without simply escaping in a flagellant nihilism. To Kerouac, Holmes was a marker, a buoy, a man on the border between straight and hip, past and present, a man with the sensitivity to make discriminations, and the openness not to fear what may have seemed bizarre to the many.

As Holmes' novels and other writings demonstrate, he is a writer who sensed and understood the social and intellectual changes catalyzing the Beats. *Go*, his first novel, captured the curious mixture of despair and new direction that enervated the lives of writers like Ginsberg (David Stofsky in the novel) and Kerouac (Gene Pasternak). Later, in *The Horn*, Holmes tried new fictional explorations into the world of jazz and hip values. These rare books – both because of their literary merits, and because they are now unfortunately out of print and as difficult to obtain as certain of Kerouac's books like *Tristessa* or *Maggie Cassidy* – inform us of what was then virtually unknown but vitally significant, the nascent stirring underground of the fifties.[1] In "The Great Rememberer" section of *Nothing More to Declare*, and in a more recent eulogistic piece which appeared in *Playboy* called "Gone in October," Holmes has done more than any other writer to define the power and person of Jack Kerouac.

During this interview – conducted in two late night sessions around a fireplace he built himself – Holmes articulates that process of definition a bit further, substituting for the elegant flourishes of stylistic evocation which writing permits with a

1 Kerouac's novels, including those unpublished in his lifetime, have been back in print since the late nineties. This interview was conducted during the years in which Kerouac's work was out of fashion.

precision of statement and perception. He sees Kerouac from a variety of vantage points: ranging from his reading habits to his technical intentions; from Kerouac's moral sense to his introverted nature and disappointed idealism. Holmes traces the ideological ramifications of the Beat movement, offering the image of a broken circuit for the sharp break in value systems that occurred during World War II, showing how the Beats' attraction to a pre-Laingian therapy of "madness," ecstasy, jazz, even criminality, were means of generating new energies in a deadening time.

I drove to Old Saybrook from New York City – normally a 2 ½ hour drive which was complicated by a fierce late March blizzard into a 7 ½ hour crawl over icy roads – and arrived at ten on a Friday night. By midnight, we began recording and did the first part of the tape. Of all the interviews I have done, this was the most organic, flowing as a discussion among willing participants along a natural course. For the rest of the weekend, I ensconced myself in Holmes' study to read his journals and his collection of over one hundred letters from Jack Kerouac, from Mexico, from Denver, from the West Coast, from Tangiers – letters which were more revealing of the literary intentions of the writer than any I had read. Late Saturday night, after a hearty stew and wine dinner, Mellon took photographs, and John Holmes gave us a tour of Old Saybrook and its vicinity. But the most enduring memory of the visit, for me, was the generous spirit, the warmth, and the hospitality of John and Shirley Holmes.

***

John Tytell: You were one of Jack Kerouac's closest friends for over twenty years. How do you account for the extreme personality changes that occurred after the publication of *On the Road*?

John Clellon Holmes: An irreconcilable division between the private self and the public life. One thing that happened to Jack was that he never understood that he had become *Jack*

Kerouac, the Marlon Brando of literature, that he had become a personality, a notoriety. He felt that people were no longer talking to him, but to an image. He knew nothing about that, cared less, and beyond that it seriously bollixed his mind.

JT: Did the fame affect his accelerated drinking?

JCH: I think so. Drink sometimes provides the illusion of single-mindedness where all the things around a problem vanish – like blinders on a horse. Of course, Jack always drank a lot, we all did in those days. But I saw him two weeks after *On the Road* came out, after Gilbert Millstein's review, and he had been on television several times, had been interviewed, and he no longer knew who the hell he was supposed to be.[2] He was temporarily discombobulated by the image of himself.

JT: Was it excitement or confusion?

JCH: When I saw him at that time, Gilbert Millstein was giving a party for him in the Village. He had invited thirty or forty people to meet this new writer. He called me because I was an old friend of Jack's. Well, Jack never showed up. At about 10:30 the phone rang, and it was Joyce Glassman, with whom he was staying then, and she asked me to speak to Jack.[3] In a quivering voice, he said, "I can't come down there. I know you've come into town to see me, and I want to see you, could you come up here?" So I went up there, and he had gone through all these interviews, and all sorts of things like girls trying to lay him, all coming suddenly in the rush of one month.

JT: After six years of anonymity, rejection, despair.

JCH: Living like a bum and feeling spiritually wasted. He had been writing things that were unacceptable in America at that time, things he clearly knew were sensational.

---

2 Millstein's rave review of On the Road for the *New York Times* effectively catapulted Kerouac into literary stardom.

3 Glassman is the maiden name of author, Joyce Johnson.

JT: Like *Visions of Cody*. It's almost unbelievable that it took so long for that book to be published in its entirety.

JCH: You can imagine the embitterment felt by anyone who could write that way and not get it published. He wasn't a primitive, but a very conscious writer.

JT: That's one of the things that William Burroughs told me that really impressed me, that Kerouac had written over a million words *before* coming to Columbia. So of course someone like that could talk about spontaneity.

JCH: He had learned his craft – it certainly shows in *The Town and The City*, which is a sort of Galsworthian family saga.

JT: When did the physical change begin?

JCH: You ought to see the kinescope of Jack's appearance with Steve Allen, whom he rather liked. He was still looking good then. He hadn't really hurt himself up to that point. He wasn't bloated or argumentative. The physical change began before he went to Big Sur in 1961. His passion had become muted, and he began to argue with himself in a way that he never had before. The Steve Allen thing was in '59 or early '60, and he still looked as I knew him back in the forties. And theoretically he was supposed to be reading from *On the Road*, but he actually read a few pages of the end of *Visions of Cody*, which he had put inside a copy of *On the Road*.

Shirley Holmes: Only you and Allen Ginsberg knew that.

JT: What can you tell me about the origins of *Visions of Cody* and how it was related to *On the Road*?

JCH: The section about Neal Cassady's boyhood was written before *On the Road*, and on pot. It's a long section that was originally published in *Playboy* about young Neal in the poolhall, and going out and catching the pass. That was intended as part of *On the Road*, written in long incredibly exfoliating sentences of great detail. At that time Sal Paradise's name was Ray Smith. Jack wrote all about his background, his getting prepared for the road, and this material was cut, and has never appeared.

JT: Wasn't that the kind of naturalistic framework he used in *The Town and The City*?

JCH: Exactly. But Jack realized that he couldn't use it in *On the Road.*

JT: Did you see the original manuscript of *On the Road*, and what were its physical properties?

JCH: I was the first person to see it, and I read it even before he did. It had no paragraphs, but it was punctuated. The names were not changed, he used real names. He didn't want to use a conventional structure because he wanted to capture the onrushing flow of his thoughts and impressions.

SH: I've always contended that Jack had this ability to go with the flow because he was such an incredible typist.

JT: John, did you visit Jack during the three-week period in which he wrote *On the Road*?

JCH: Yes. Recently, I had occasion to examine my journals, which you'll read tomorrow. I had an entry in early April, 1951, of going down to see Jack, who was living in Chelsea with Joan Haverty, and by that day, I think it was the ninth of April, he had written 34,000 words. The long roll of what looked to me like shelf paper was spread out on the floor in front of the typewriter. I found another entry on April 27th when he delivered the book to me. He had finished it two days before, a huge thick roll, and he said he hadn't read it yet. I spent the entire day reading it, and it was almost a third longer than the published version.

JT: Malcolm Cowley says that he suggested a lot of the trips be eliminated to create greater focus.[4]

4 Cowley, one of America's best known literary editors, worked with Viking Press and encouraged them to publish Kerouac's novel.

JCH: Jack did a lot of this even before Cowley suggested it. He had a lot of material on the terminal points like New York and San Francisco, and took them out because they didn't relate to the road experience. When Jack typed the novel in pages, he made numerous changes – he always made more changes than he would ever admit to – and submitted it to Harcourt, Brace, and it was rejected. This was quite a blow to him. So I said, let me take it to my agent – he didn't even have an agent then, but was working strictly through Giroux – to M.C.A. and my agent then, Rae Everitt, now Rae Brooks, and she didn't fully appreciate it, but told Jack a few things which he sensibly ignored. Jack was sobered by the rejection though, depressed is not the word. He had to really think about himself and what he wanted to do. He had already had part of this experience in realizing he couldn't write *On the Road* in the way he had done *The Town and The City*, that he had to abandon the idea of family structures and just set his characters free in the country. What he started to do almost immediately is what he called sketching; that is, looking in windows, observing the street, and taking it down at the time it was happening.

JT: Direct notation rather than recalled notation.

JCH: Rather than trying to *give* a shape, trying to existentially discover it, as in the beginning of *Visions of Cody*. He told me he never thought of this as being publishable. He was simply trying to catch the flow. He had felt from the beginning that something in Neal had eluded him. Jack had an enormous capacity for saying, "Everything I've done so far is lies." While writing *On the Road* he said he was writing it because *The Town and The City* was a lie, a fiction. *On the Road* was to tell the story as it was, but afterwards Jack felt he still hadn't caught the idea of Neal, so he began *Visions of Cody*, which he didn't conceive as a structured book, but more an expansion of his imaginative conception of Neal.

JT: So it led to a series of extensions, projections, and games based on Neal which captures him more internally somehow.

JCH: It's closer to Neal, but ultimately very mythic. I've always thought that the picture of Neal in *On the Road* is dramatically better, but the character is not as monumental as in *Visions of Cody*. What Jack did was invent a plethora of new techniques for *Visions of Cody* because he couldn't create the character he wanted if he remained outside him.

JT: *Visions of Cody*, for me, is when Kerouac really comes into his own. *Dr. Sax* also has that sense of inventive leaping, that unique power and freedom of form.

JCH: Obviously Jack was searching to free himself from all the novelistic necessities as they existed then in order to freely sing, not as in *The Town and The City* where the songs were more or less set pieces, recitatives, or arias. What he wanted to do was employ the totality of his feeling, sensibility, and erudition, and make it part of the flow he was describing. This is why he was always so close to [James] Joyce – a deep passion of his I never particularly shared. He wanted, as Joyce did, simultaneity; Jack not only wanted to describe something – which he did better than anyone I've ever known – but also to embody it with everything about himself and his feelings that he could get into it. And he wanted to find a way in which all of this could flow together. Jack would never have claimed it, but it seems to me that the real engine behind the English in *Cody* is Shakespeare. There are sections of *Cody* which are as eloquent as any prose I've ever read.

JT: It is interesting that Shakespeare, Joyce, and Kerouac are all freed of certain inhibitions of syntax and style and structure, and as a result can perfect a powerful flow, anarchically, freely.

JCH: It happens when the image finds the word or words immediately, and you don't stop to think, "Is it working?" You just plunge on. That's why there are lines in Kerouac that you must flow with to understand; the moment you stop to conceptualize they break down. But what gets into line is a whole series of tumultuous impressions and takes that can only be compared to film, and Jack, of course, was very affected by film. Also, Jack spoke French before he spoke English, and like many people who work in a language not their own, he was very sensitive to it. Jack was a word man all the way, and had a veneration for language – which is why he loved Joyce.

JT: He seems, judging from his letters, to have read a lot.

JCH: He was a tremendously well-read man. He read erratically, but deeply, and when he read something he never forgot it.

JT: I've read letters that Jack wrote to Allen Ginsberg when Jack had already left Columbia but was still reading as if he were still there, five, seven, ten huge books a week. Not all of them necessarily, parts of Pascal, of the Bible, *Moby Dick* in a day or two.

JCH: He had an amazing memory for what he had read. He would often come here because I had most of Balzac, and I suppose that any writer who is writing a saga thinks of Balzac, as Faulkner did. Jack loved Balzac, and came here because he felt it was quiet enough, and he would pile Balzac next to that chair and read him for a week. Then years later he would make some reference to one of the fifty-odd novels by Balzac that I have. So read and remembered.

JT: Do you know whether he read Henry Miller, or ever expressed any attitudes towards Miller's work?

JCH: Frankly, no. But I had read Miller early, and approved of him as I approved of what I then thought of as good dirty-book writers. I was attracted to Lawrence and Miller in my teens, and managed to read the forbidden Miller in my early twenties. Now Jack loved Lawrence almost despite his reputation, but I never remember him saying anything about Miller until the mid-fifties.

JT: That's interesting because it seems to me that Miller

started something that Jack continued, and that was writing a saga about yourself. Miller, of course, did that remarkable Preface for *The Subterraneans*.

JCH: Jack must have been pleased by the effort of an older writer to help him along, and to recognize him, but I know that Jack didn't see Miller even though a meeting was planned. I believe Miller is a great American writer. When anybody really reads what he has done, any idea that he is simply prurient or pornographic is utterly ridiculous. He's in a deep American tradition.

JT: During the years after writing *On the Road*, from 1951 until its publication in 1957, how much of Kerouac did you see?

JCH: I saw him only intermittently because he was in Mexico and on the West Coast. We saw each other whenever he came back to New York. When he was gone we corresponded, and he sent me all his manuscripts during those years. That is, up to '54-'55 when he went to San Francisco and everything started to happen. They all came back here – Jack, Allen, Peter on their way to North Africa – and they were up here around New Year's of '57. Viking was going to publish *On the Road*, and we spent a whole week up here just getting to know one another again, and Jack was still very much the way he had been before. He'd been on the mountain and written the first half of *Desolation Angels*. He had also written the first part of *Tristessa*, which I read then too.

JT: How had he sent you the other books, like *Dr. Sax*?

JCH: In the mail. He would send me the originals, and I turned them all over to an agent, or to Allen, or to Carl Solomon. The original *Dr. Sax* went to Carl who was then working for A.A. Wyn, his uncle, who wouldn't publish it.

JT: The book probably didn't seem commercially feasible to Wyn.

JCH: Carl wanted it published, he was fighting for certain

things with Wyn, but they were a very small house. Carl got through that Jaime de Angulo book, *Indian Tales*, which has become a classic, and he got a few others like *Junkie* through. This must have been an enormous source of pressure on Carl. He knew what was good, what would become important, but he was working nine to five. I used to meet him for lunch then. He had his problems anyway, and to fight the publisher's bullshit all the time, when there was no recognition that it was shit anywhere… Listen, you couldn't even wrap yourself in the American flag and say, "I'm going down for integrity and how about that, baby!" because the books he wanted to accept were considered filthy – you were considered some kind of a fruitcake to believe they were good. But those were awful years. You've treated it so well in that one section of your book that I've read on the fifties.

JT: I was in high school and college at the end of the fifties, and I felt it.

JCH: You must have, because you describe it brilliantly. You felt like you were fighting a hopeless battle against everything. One reason why Jack and Allen, and the rest of us, have not been upset by the new freedom is that we know what it came from. We were serious writers, and we earned every "fuck" we wrote down. Take *Go*, for instance. I used no four-letter words except at one point, he comes out onto the street after a party and something has happened – indeed Allen Ginsberg has been arrested – and he says "Fuck you! Fuck you! Fuck you! Fuck you! Fuck you! Fuck you!" - six times. Scribner's lawyer asked me to cut out three of these, and I said, "If I can publish three, I can do six. I'm trying to make a point here: the man is out of control." But that was characteristic of the circumstances under which you worked then. They said, "Can't you change it to 'fug'?" Mailer had done that, but I refused and insisted that it had to be six "Fuck you!"s – it had nothing to do with sex, or dirty words, it had to do with despair. But they thought quantitatively then, and that's one reason why *Visions of Cody* couldn't come out. Now Jack was a very moral, almost puritanical person, but he used the language of eroticism when it seemed right.

JT: That's interesting. I've felt that when Kerouac treats women in his fiction that moral sense creates a false distance making the women less real, more romanticized than he might have realized or intended.

JCH: Well, this was certainly not entirely due to the literary restrictions of the time. He did tend to idealize women.

JT: You can see it in *Tristessa*, for example, where you have a woman named Esmeralda in real life – hope in Spanish – who is a drug addict and a whore, but whom he transforms into a Mary Magdalene, a saint of the streets. He does capture her desolation, but still there is such a pedestal quality, almost a worship of her suffering.

JCH: This relates to something larger that Jack tended to idealize. He plunged deeply into the stuff of life in his time, and – it's hard to say whether he was educated by it or disappointed – he had an enormous ability to empathize with human beings. He was a person who stood off from life to a degree that is not recognized. He was not deeply involved, he was not part of the swirl, he was not dancing on the floor or driving the car, he was not swinging.

JT: Ann Charters relates how withdrawn he was at parties, always standing apart.[5]

JCH: To some degree this may be true of artists generally, but it was pronounced in him. I have seen him in the center of things, but this was the exception. This is where drink came in, because it connected him to the outside, but by himself he was serious, grave, not a drag, but hard to engage. He was a man who felt at a distance from most people, and he was aware of this all the time because of his own hunger to cross it, and this is what made him a difficult person for some people to communicate with because he didn't seem to be there all the

5 Charters was the author of the first Kerouac biography.

time. He was a brooding presence. Then he would get drunk or high, and he would be the most gregarious person you ever met, the most charming and attractive, the most imaginative man I've ever known, just a continuous flow of fantasy, ideas, funny nothings, and weird images. But he was driven. He was a man who sat completely inside his own consciousness and never, or rarely, got out of that envelope. And he accepted this, and followed it wherever it led, but it was often into things that were debilitating for him. He had a very fatalistic sense of himself, and to me he was a genius, whatever that word means. I've only met one, and I know many people who are extremely talented, and kinetic, and everything else. But ultimately, Jack had a mystery inside him that I never could penetrate at all, and I don't think he ever could either. I think Allen would confirm this.

JT: And at the heart of him was the energy of his imaginative facility. How would you characterize it?

JCH: Jack would constantly come up with things: titles, ideas, takes – often he wouldn't follow them up, but the constant spew…

JT: Like the title for "Howl," *Naked Lunch*, *Big Table*?

JCH: It was that he would read something and do a take on it, and sometimes it seemed outrageous, mean or bitter, indifferent or too enthusiastic, but it always had some sense to it that often would come out later. About eight years before he died I stopped questioning him – that is, I stopped saying, "Oh Jack, you're full of shit!" I would often say it, but I gradually stopped believing it because there was always an odd kind of prophetic logic to the way he thought, even when he was fumed with booze. Like he wrote a thing for *Escapade* – he was something of a right-winger, you know – on Khrushchev whom he had seen getting off a plane in Washington, having to stand in the sun during speeches, enduring the passing of the Marine band, a sixty year old man sweating with his hat off, and Jack, who hated Communism, wrote in this tit magazine, “I demand justice for this man Khrushchev.” And this was typical of Jack who sympathized with the man, any man undergoing the experience of the moment. He related to that.

JT: Even though Jack writes about working-class characters like Neal, exulting, for example, in the power with which Neal could change tires, there doesn’t seem to be any sense of class conflict or awareness in his fiction such as you might find in a more political writer like Dos Passos. He goes right to the man because of something central in his subject’s experience.

JCH: Still, there was this definite class feeling in Jack, although it was almost always on the surface. Show him the human situation and if it was clear enough to him, that’s what he would reach for. That’s really what the whole Beat thing was about. It was kind of an American existentialism – it said don’t talk to me about excuses but show me what’s happening.

JT: How does that work in with class though?

JCH: It doesn’t, of course. But what I’m trying to say is that Jack, when he was not creatively engaged, thought very much about class – not intelligently, he didn’t write much about it – but he was full of class resentment. He who seemed to me to be so brilliant, nevertheless resented people who had more education than he did, more privilege, more money.

JT: Do you think this might have had its origin in the experience of attending Horace Mann, and then Columbia, as a young man from a provincial town without any kind of support?

JCH: Undoubtedly. That must have been a factor. It always seemed to me, knowing Jack, and even more in reading his work, that he always felt separate, he even felt separate from his family and the immediate background which gave him his material. He felt special, isolated, lonely, and this never changed.

JT: The feeling I have about all of these figures is the spiritual state of exile, not that one has to – like Burroughs – leave the country or expatriate, but in the sense of Stephen Dedaelus' exile which is all the more profound for being within one's own family and country.[6]

JCH: Well, the Beat thing begins with the feeling of difference.

JT: And outcast, or self-outcast as a result?

JCH: Well, at first Jack wanted to be like his father. He started being nostalgic about life in Lowell when he was seventeen, perhaps even earlier. But he never felt part of it. He was like Rimbaud.

JT: His poem on Rimbaud is probably the best place to begin when looking for what motivated the Beat experience. In *The Town and The City*, when Levinsky first appears, he is carrying a volume of Rimbaud.

JCH: It is so difficult to speak about it sociologically, but what had happened in the late thirties and early forties was a kind of uprootedness in terms of family relationships. The whole society was changing, and a major event was about to happen, and everybody knew it, particularly young men. And it was also clear that all the ways by which people had understood an event like this in the past were inadequate.

JT: And isn't what you are attempting to describe exactly the context of *The Town and The City* where both family ties and community allegiance lose their validity in the face of some looming threat? The sense of imminent devastation for young men – almost Hemingway's theme.

JCH: Right, but what it did with Jack and all of us to some degree was to make more poignant the things that had been

6 Dedaelus, James Joyce's literary alter-ego, which inspired Kerouac's own pseudonym, Duloz.

lost. You allude to this in one of your essays when you refer to the deep conservative element in all this. It set Jack thinking about families; it set me thinking about marriage, love, cohesiveness, and more than that – continuity. Ginsberg is relentlessly writing about continuity, or its absence, but what nerves all of Allen's work is the broken circuit, and the broken circuit is in Jack's work all the way.

JT: That's a good image.

JCH: So we issued out of the war into a cultural scene, the dominant tone of which was irony and craft, Henry James and Auden.

JT: Containment and form.

JCH: And caution. Don't spit it out. And this is what made Allen erupt, "I saw the best minds of my generation destroyed by madness…" which he has been laughed at for writing, but which is so true, and this is what made Jack write, "The only people for me are the mad ones," in *On the Road*. And what moves both passages is that they are both saying there's a break, there's a terrible break that has occurred: I have known those who have been destroyed by it, I believe in people who are trying to mend. Now these lines were done independently of each other, but they really epitomize what this whole thing was about.

***

JT: Last night we were talking about the importance of madness as motivation in Ginsberg's work, and in Kerouac's work, and the fact that from their point of view the madness that they pursued was not madness but the only way to move, to see the society and deal with it, and that stance leading to a whole reinterpretation of the relativity of madness.

JCH: Yes. If you accept the modern world on its terms, and

are content with it, then anyone who can't function in it is strange, bent, twisted, etc., but one of the qualities in the Beat movement was the recognition that madness was a kind of retreat for those who wanted to stay privately sane. We understood that madness meant pain, as any withdrawal does, but the idea that there was any way to formulate social sanity was one of the things that we tried to give up, just as we tried to give up Freudianism, Marxism, and all determinisms. And everyone knew people who went mad, or felt themselves going mad sometimes – that is, getting physically out of step with the world – and all too often it was because of a different standard that the world continually abused. So people broke down because of this dichotomy; in other words, it's early Laing.[7] This was certainly true of Allen who was put in Columbia Psychiatric Institute because of things completely outside him. His apartment was full of stolen goods brought there by Huncke and the two others living there.

JT: Lionel Trilling explained to me that Allen went to P.I. as a result of a deal with the District Attorney, Frank Hogan, who was a Columbia University graduate, and who agreed to allow Allen to serve time in a psychiatric ward rather than a penal ward. Actually, as Laing and Thomas Szasz have argued, it is much the same thing though.

JCH: But what happened with Allen while he was there was interesting – since he ultimately confused the analysts by being saner than they were. He was more honest for one thing, so they said they couldn't do anything for him.

JT: That's another aspect of something Carl Solomon told me – that he felt in his life there was a danger of talking his way into the institution. So honest is a twisting key itself. But in the culture of the late forties and early fifties, the nature of madness was almost an idea that Norman O. Brown discusses in *Life Against Death*, that the greatest madness lies in resisting one's natural inclinations to madness, so that

7 R.D. Laing (1927-1989), Scottish psychiatrist who wrote extensively on the subject of psychosis.

from that point of view you can see the sense of control of a Nixon as being the archetype of madness in our day. Maybe that's what leads to war.

JCH: Allen would say, and I would agree with him, as Blake said, that anything that comes directly from the inner self is good, it sweats, it's real. Being disembodied is really being mad.

JT: Not being in touch with oneself – what Laing calls "ontological insecurity."

JCH: Talking like a gramophone like Nixon talks, simply mouthing things, talking out of a dream, an MGM fantasy.

JT: Yes, like the time he reputedly appeared at the Washington Monument before a peace rally at 5am and addressed a small group as if he was in a trance.

JCH: Certain kinds of clichés are the narcotics of the middle class, and Nixon plays on these automatically. I think he really believes these things so I can't hate him. He's so removed that he is sad to me, not loathsome. But he is everything that we have to recoil from, and I mean spiritually, not just politically.

JT: Was there any general attitude among the Beats towards psychoanalysis? I know Burroughs went through it, and disdains it now. How did Kerouac feel about it?

JCH: Well, Jack had an experience in the Navy where he was discharged, I forget the phrase they used…

JT: "Paranoid schizophrenic." In one of his letters, he says they added "paranoid" to his diagnosis because he was intelligent.

JCH: Well, that about sums it up. In other words, we all felt that psychoanalysis was an inadequate description of human activity. It just couldn't go far enough, the way that sociology also failed to include the spirit or mystery, and that's what we were after. It really didn't help to know that you had a father complex or a mother complex. The Beat attitude amounted to more than that. We felt that this approach was as oversimplified as Marx's understanding of class relations. The attitude, to call it that, was protesting against what we felt was an inadequate conception of the nature of man. In 1945, man was seen as a victim, either of toilet training or his place in society, because he was determined from the outside. That conception of man we all found, quite independently because we all have different backgrounds, to be increasingly inadequate. We felt that there had to be something more. Thoreau talks about it, and Emerson, and we found that the deepest strain in American politics and poetry to be metaphysical. The American Constitution starts out by enunciating certain inalienable rights; no European had ever conceived of that – that certain rights are innate! When the French began talking about the rights of man it led to the rolling of heads. But we began by defining man as free, and our experiment worked because our variety, our difference, our lack of homogeneity meant that every one of us had to become Americans, which meant becoming new men – it was no birthright. Everyone except the Indians came from somewhere else. So primarily we are a passionately political people and politics is our church, the thing that holds us together as both Whitman and Lincoln used to say. Well, we wander afield a bit.

JT: I'd like to wander in another direction – the importance of jazz music to the Beats. For example, Allen today writing and singing a poetic based on blues, or earlier this afternoon, I was reading in your journals an entry describing a party in 1951 where Allen was singing blues, improvising rhymes to fit the people present at the party. The same interest is certainly evident in Kerouac's work, and in your novel, *The Horn*. What do you think caused this general interest?

JCH: Well, young people in America, at least in the last three generations, have felt music as a very important part of their lives: In the thirties it was swing, in the late forties it was bop, then rock. American music – jazz, blues, it all comes from a black base – has in our century seemed to young people to express all sorts of inexpressible exuberance and energy. Now with Jack and me and Allen and others of that time I suppose jazz meant more than that. Fed up as we were with trite explanations of why things happened, and with an attitude towards the world that also seemed inadequate, jazz was a call from the dark, it was a euphoria of joy, dance, let loose. Also, everyone at that time believed that blacks knew something that we didn't know, only because they appeared less surface-worried than we were.

JT: Mailer writes about that in "The White Negro" – about learning a model of experience and the courage to face the world from the black man.

JCH: You can sum it up like this. When Jack wrote about walking in the Denver black section in *On the Road*, James Baldwin said he'd love to hear Jack reading that in the Apollo Theater in New York because Jack would get crucified. Less than ten years later, Eldridge Cleaver praised that section as an early sign of a new liberated consciousness. So whether we were deluded or not, what we wanted was that untrammeled swing and style that blacks, undoubtedly as a defense, had created. Also because *we* felt like blacks caught in the square world that wasn't enough for us, and we felt that blacks had more immediate fun than we did.

JT: Do you feel that the Beats had a greater sense of the street than writers have had previously, even the Naturalists? I'm thinking of figures like Huncke or Neal.

JCH: Absolutely. We knew that street knowledge meant functioning in the world, so what writer wouldn't be interested in talking to a man like Huncke? We went to Huncke like you might go to Dostoevski just because of the kind of life he had lived – he was a source – even more, a model of how to survive. That was part of the appeal Neal had for Jack, because had answered questions Jack couldn't answer for himself, or so Jack fancied it. All of Jack's work was motivated by a disappointed idealism, and Neal presented an answer to the break that Jack felt in himself. I once saw Neal look at Jack, and I imagined I saw in Neal's face, "You're not seeing me anymore, you're seeing only your idea," because Neal was a man who had literal day to day problems.

JT: So Huncke told me: "He was a nervous cat all the time!"

JCH: Right. He was as hung up with women problems, transportation problems as any of the rest of us, but Jack increasingly saw him as a kind of hero who was being brought down by the necessities of square life. Jack was never unaware of the domestic bullshit in Neal's life.

JT: He had to be aware of it because he lived with Neal and Carolyn several times, and left on one occasion because he could no longer stand Neal's peculiar games. In *Big Sur*, however, Kerouac implies that Neal felt exploited, that his life had been used. I mean at the end of the novel when Neal stands in the doorway in a golden light – which for Kerouac signified a moment of annunciation – as Jack unwraps copies of *On the Road* which have just arrived, and Neal looks away, unable to look into Jack's eyes.

JCH: I was reasonably close to Neal, and always liked him, and I've often thought about what *On the Road* must have done to him as a man, you know the idea that he had become a myth in his own time, because he wasn't a mythic character – he was simply a fascinating human being. So when Jack gained his recognition after *On the Road*, okay, Jack had at least written a book, but Neal suddenly became a figure quite by happenstance, and it got more and more complicated as Jack's works appeared. Jack was always deadly honest in his work. Not always in his life but always in his work. So that episode near the end of *Big Sur* is revealing. I agree with you.

JT: You said that Neal didn't have a mythic presence, but it is curious to me that after leaving Jack's orbit Neal goes to Kesey, suddenly appears in Kesey's backyard, and that started the friendship that led to the Merry Pranksters. But the point is that Neal sought Kesey out as one man of power seeks another.

JCH: Well, Neal liked people who liked him.

JT: Also, to put it vulgarly, he knew where the action was almost instinctively – I think because of that remarkable street sense that he had.

JCH: Definitely. Neal was one of the most street-wise men I ever met.

JT: And sophisticated in certain ways at the same time, and the wonder of it to me – although it fits so perfectly into the American tradition – is that it is all so self-learned.

JCH: The most sophisticated people are those who have never read books, or gone to school, but just lived their lives intensely. Huncke is ones of the most sophisticated men I've ever met. What is sophistication? It's knowing how things work, where things are, keeping all the elements separate and knowing how to handle them.

JT: That's the way Rojack in Mailer's *An American Dream* defines sanity: keeping in your mind the maximum number of impossible combinations.

JCH: Neal certainly knew that. Besides, as you say, he wanted action and knew how to get it. But with Kesey everything accelerated – the stakes were higher, the drugs different, like LSD.

JT: Right. Neal had spent two years in San Quentin for giving two plainclothesmen a marijuana cigarette, and now he was driving a communal freak bus for Kesey and they were all distributing acid. It is like the magnified end of a cycle beginning maybe when Huncke, Burroughs, and Neal drove back from New Waverly to New York City in '47 with a jeep full of marijuana that they had harvested and put in mason jars. And before that Bill Garver's stealing overcoats around Times Square to support his habit, or Huncke hustling, breaking and entering with Little Jack Melody, Neal's reputed theft of over five hundred automobiles mostly for joy-rides in the Denver hills when he was still really just a kid. All of which leads to another question: what was the attraction of the underworld and the lifestyle of the criminal? With Burroughs, for example, beginning with a Gidean devotion and fascination. Also, his whole notion of the relativity of legality which is expressed in letters to Allen that I've read up at Columbia University where Burroughs comments, for instance, on the wetback situation in Texas where he was farming in '47 – how large farmers are allowed to get away with it, while smaller farmers can't, and how anyway the wetbacks are profiting since they could earn three to eight dollars a day instead of fifty cents a day in Mexican fields. Yet at the same time they are treated as slaves, and if they didn't pick cotton, could be shot in the fields, while the U.S. authorities encourage the large growers since there is no other way to harvest. So the whole question of what law is becomes itself in question, or it becomes an economic class determinant more than an ethical determinant.

JCH: True. It seems that our attraction to criminality, mostly crimes without a victim like drugs, fits in with our feeling that the definition of man's nature was inadequate. And we were interested in excessive experiences, in the extreme, because a man who puts himself outside the law is a man who is putting himself *into* himself – he's said okay, I'll go alone, and we were fascinated with this because then a man has nothing to depend on except what's inside him.

JT: I noticed a picture of Norman Mailer in that group of about thirty pictures of writers in your study. When was that taken?

JCH: Early sixties. It was when he did a thing for *Esquire* about writers and the bitch goddess, and they shot him in a ring with a hand over each rope, and it struck me then as summing up the only Mailer I've ever known, at once aggressive and perceptive.

JT: What was Mailer's reaction to the Beat movement?

JCH: He became sympathetic to it starting about 1957. Somewhere around then in his column for *The Village Voice* he got into the conflict between hip and square and predicted that the choice between these positions would be the real problem for Americans for the next twenty-five years. Now when I knew Norman in 1952 or '53, he knew nothing about this and didn't much care. He was a Trotskyite. But the hip/square columns had to do, I think, with something relating to *The Deer Park*, that never quite got into *The Deer Park*. He suddenly had a vision of all this – he hadn't been really paying any attention, and he hadn't been on the street or he would have known. He had found success very young, and had a more or less concretized way of thinking about things.

SH: And he had a very sneering attitude towards the Beat thing at parties.

JCH: Well, not exactly. I remember a party at Vance [Bourjaily]'s right after *On the Road* came out, and Mailer took me into a corner and said, "Tell me everything you know about Kerouac!" And when Norman met Jack, he liked him. But Norman had to run out of all the intellectual disciplines by which he had motivated his work before he came to the dark night of the soul. The inner life broke in on him because everything else ran out.

JT: Maybe because he was really receptive as well. He did offer *Naked Lunch* its first most significant praise.

JCH: The thing that makes Mailer for me a very great writer is that he follows his nose wherever it goes. We all know about *Naked and the Dead. Barbary Shore* was a really serious attempt to write the first existentialist novel in America, but what it resulted in was that Norman was rubbed raw. *The Deer Park* was his first attempt to do something where he didn't quite know what he was doing.

JT: And Sergius O'Shaugnessy, in a subsequent story, "The Time of Her Time," one of the great sex stories of all time, does finally make that transition from square to hip, from Hemingway's "Lost Generation" consciousness to a glimmer of beatness.

JCH: But imagine what Norman had to go through to make Sergius do that. He had to be willing to experience it himself first. That is, Norman is the guy who wanted to be like Thomas Wolfe and others – when their books were published people ran right out and bought them. He had the same hope that we all had that the publication of a new book by a certain writer would be an event. We all had to learn that that simply wasn't true anymore. It had nothing to do with money, but whether literature meant anything any longer. So Norman is the only writer I know who made himself into a celebrity by a conscious effort, and enormous sacrifice. To me it has sometimes seemed a waste of energy.

JT: I wanted to ask you what you thought of Mailer's idea in "The White Negro" that a certain quality of pathology is necessary to heroism in our time, and especially becomes the natural response to an encroaching totalitarianism, and what did such an attitude have to do with the whole question of rebellion in the Beat movement? You know, the fact that you were not just going to accept the given conditions, and you were all seeking another way, of conducting your lives with the kind of joy and illusion of freedom that Mailer attributes to the blacks in "The White Negro." So a kind of craziness, or a pathological response, or what society would have seen as a violation of its code of adjustment and acceptance, and therefore termed crazy, which in turn only means that a society has the power to intern you in a certain kind of prison.

JCH: I think we denied the ready-made explanations for human behavior, and we were drawn to aspects of human experience that were ignored by all the sciences or condemned by society.

JT: And apparently, reading the letters describing the parties of the late forties, you were all very drawn to the idea of breaking control and getting out of one's ordinary head, partly for joy, partly for the sake of new perception. In this connection, I wanted to ask you about Jack's friend, Bill Cannastra. What period was that?

JCH: He died in 1950, in a revealing manner. He was on a subway, a local train, somewhere downtown, and as the train pulled out of a stop – the windows were open because it was warm – he tried to get out through the open window, was about halfway out as the train gathered speed, and struck a pillar. He was very athletic: he climbed up fire escapes and dangled himself over the sides of buildings and so forth, but he was just drunk. The girl he was with claimed that he said, "I'm going to go get a drink." Maybe it was just claustrophobia or boredom.

JT: How would you characterize him? How well did you know him?

JCH: I knew him pretty well. One reason that I put him into *Go* was that he seemed a contrast to Neal, Jack, and the rest of us. He was an alcoholic; his motivation was embitteredness, the world's approaching end. His way of playing was self-destructive, it was giving wild parties that went on for days, and which were not chic at all but raunchy – we all dug ugliness then, that is, the worse it was, the more interesting it seemed to be. Cannastra would do anything: humiliate people, usually himself first, you know, take off all his clothes and fart, scream, and yell. He seemed to be somebody playing on the edge, and he appealed to me because I was moving into a new world which didn't demand that one be a victim as he was. He thought of himself as having seen the lie of life, and responded to it like Rochester did – I mean the poet – by saying, "Anything goes now because it's all rotten anyway."[8]

8 John Wilmot (1647-1680), Second Earl of Rochester.

Now I felt like that then, but I was changing over to the feeling that something in the streets could be found that was more interesting than this.

JT: Did he work?

JCH: He was a graduate of Harvard Law School who had abandoned his practice. At that point he was a bisexual drunk who lived in a loft in Chelsea, and did everyday jobs like working in a bakery. He couldn't have been more than thirty when he died. He was an outrageous man, and I liked him because he was outrageous. He used to go into bars in Chelsea or near the docks and give longshoremen big wet tongue kisses, and say, "Buy me a drink," and they would beat him up, but then buy him drinks because he wasn't a "pansy," only premature-Camp.

JT: Did you know Jerry Newman? Allen Ginsberg told me that he did a radio bit called "The Drunken Newscaster" that Burroughs heard which may have influenced the idea of the cut-up.

JCH: I knew him, but nothing about that. When I first met him he had a record shop off Eighth Street west of Sixth Avenue, and then he started a record company called Esoteric. Jack had known him at Horace Mann, and they shared a common passion for jazz in the early years of World War II. One of the first things he did was to record that marvelous serenade by Schonberg. It was just the beginning of LPs. He knew little about Schonberg, but he had a perfect ear, and he made this performance by editing different tapes. This is common practice now, but he was one of the first to get a final product by editing several different versions.

JT: When did you take courses at the New School for Social Research with Kerouac?

JCH: It was in the fall of '49, more than a year after the initial meeting I describe in *Nothing More to Declare*. Both of us had G.I. benefits left, so even though *The Town and The City* was coming out we decided it was ridiculous not to take advantage of the year we were still entitled to, plus they gave you some living money every month and free books.

JT: What courses did you take?

JCH: We took some courses in common, like the Meyer Shapiro course about the Impressionists. It was a huge class so there was no real interchange, but he was an inspiring teacher. We both sat in on a course that Alfred Kazin was giving on *Moby Dick*, and he was a brilliant teacher, too. I took a medieval literature course, and a comparative religion course, and we both started a myth course with Harry Slochower but only attended about two classes. He was a bore with a Marxist viewpoint who treated myth like merchandise.

JT: In *Nothing More to Declare* you mention that Kerouac once tried to screw the earth. That sounds like something that might happen in the excesses of a D.H. Lawrence novel. Was it a literal episode?

JCH: Yes. It was while he was writing *The Town and The City*. I heard it from him, and read it in his journals of the time. He was trying to write, and he was alone, and horny, and young, and so he thumbed a hole in his backyard, and he fucked the earth. He had lots of Lawrencian feelings anyway.

JT: We were talking this morning about Jack's humor which has been unappreciated in his work and in his life. Did that exuberance diminish as you got to know him?

JCH: Seeing the funny side of things comes from a certain distance and an ironical way of looking at life. Jack didn't have this naturally, but he loved good fun. He was terribly amused by his own work sometimes, and as you pointed out when he reads certain things, like some of the poems, he reads them as if they were funny because they were to him. But I wouldn't say that he saw things comedically. He saw things fondly, he loved human folly and silliness, he responded to anything that had a pathetic element in it in a very endearing way.

JT: Like the great flyswatter episode in *Visions of Cody* where Neal, as a child, watches his father and another Bowery wino travel to Nebraska farms selling these ridiculous flyswatters.

JCH: Well, Jack had a great sense of the absurd.

JT: But isn't that one of the uniquely differentiating qualities about Kerouac as a writer: he is one of the very few who have any warmth left in his sense of humor, as opposed to the way most writers use humor as a devastating social castigation.

JCH: That's why Jack didn't like Lenny Bruce – he couldn't stand anything that appeared to demean human beings. He was a bridge-builder; he felt some wound had occurred in the contemporary soul, and he was trying to suggest how it could be mended. One of the oldest functions of literature, after all.

The Joyous Disease

In 1955, Jack Kerouac wrote Allen Ginsberg that three of his favorite writers ended up as recluses – Blake, Thoreau, and Emily Dickenson. I think he was predicting his own future, but the perspective of the recluse, a bitter contradiction of the genuine warmth and compassion of his best fiction, certainly colors his views of America during his last years.

Kerouac's final take on his own country must be measured by the fact that he was first of all a poet who used the novel as his form. The terms of his last views are blurred by what he called "the joyous disease," the alcoholism that reamed him out at the end, which may have been the only solace for the loss of an enormous talent. Great American novelists do have peak periods: think of Melville in the early 1850s, Faulkner in the early 1930s, or Jack Kerouac in the early 1950s. Kerouac himself was fully aware of this, and in 1952 he exclaimed in a letter that "I have completely reached my peak maturity now and am blowing such mad poetry and literature that I'll look back years later with amazement and chagrin that I can't do it anymore."

What does the loss of such power imply for any artist who has glimpsed its intoxicating flights? Kerouac's emotional decline corresponds with his own awareness that he could no longer match his earlier inspirations. Like Henry Miller, Kerouac had a prodigious exuberance that often resulted in extremely prolific writing sessions that could produce up to five thousand words. In his early journals, like some Ben Franklin or Horatio Alger, he measured his daily output with a batting average. We often take the writer's effort for granted, and those of us who are not writers cannot know how depleting the work can be. Conrad or Hemingway, for example, would be mentally exhausted after five hundred words.

Henry Miller, who did his great work in Paris in the *Tropics* novels in the 1930s, had little inclination to continue writing when he returned to America after the war. He was more or less cajoled into *The Rosy Crucifixion*, a tepid retelling of the *Tropics* material, by Janine Lepska, his third wife, who thought her husband should be writing. Something of a similar nature occurred to Kerouac after the success of *On the Road* when his publishers asked for a sequel, which he gave them with *The Dharma Bums*. But *On the Road* had been written six years before its appearance in 1957, and Kerouac had already lost much of his power. On some level he had to be aware of this diminution.

The best account of this mysterious change is provided by Kerouac's friend, John Clellon Holmes. In 1951, when Kerouac finished the marathon three-week literary explosion that resulted in the scroll manuscript of *On the Road*, he brought it to Holmes to read. Holmes was astounded by what he regarded as a major formal breakthrough. Kerouac's novel was rejected by several publishers, mostly because of his unorthodox manuscript and his refusal to consider revisions, and that stand nearly cost him his entire literary career. Imagine how he felt when Holmes' forced and flat version of *On the Road* appeared in 1953.

It is a sign of Kerouac's extraordinary generosity that he forgave his friend and continued to see him until the end of his life. When interviewing Holmes in his home in Old Saybrook, Connecticut, in 1974, I read in his journals the most convincing account of Kerouac's notorious decline into a soured, mean-spirited, often delirious incoherence, a shriveling bitterness that precipitated his early death at the age of forty-seven.

Kerouac stayed at Holmes' Old Saybrook home in the fall of 1962, while Kerouac was ostensibly house searching. Actually, during the last decade of his life – as a register of his personal confusion – he had relocated with his mother from Northport, Long Island, to Lowell, to California, and to St. Petersburg, Florida.

In the fourth day of the visit, Holmes noted that Kerouac was already up and drinking Courvoisier at nine. By afternoon, Kerouac was napping:

> that incredible, lava-hot flow of memories, imaginations, perceptions, nonsense and humor temporarily stilled. We ranted and argued… and I've been close to that unapproachable core again, and I actually think that he has a good time. He is probably the most prodigious, indefatigable drinker I've ever known. His genius is exhausting, unique, volcanic, and is fed somehow by booze… his strange amalgam of spurious ideas, verbal illumination, cornball politics, dead certain aesthetic feeling, huge relish for life, fatalistic physical strength – all that I knew so well has at once come back to me in a rush. The horrors

> lie ahead for him tomorrow or Saturday, he knows it (having that queer strain of self-knowledge that is part of all real talents in our time). Our feelings towards one another remain ambiguous. We like one another enormously, we are so utterly different and disagree with great foaming screams. Anyway, I'm enjoying these wasteful, abusive days of literally hours and hours of frantic, drunken talk – one flowing into the other, all sequence and cohesion swept away sometime days and days ago. I try to keep shaved and reasonably sweet-smelling. Jack sits down in torn blue pajama bottoms, a rank tee shirt, grimy socks and Japanese slippers, unshaven in nearly a week, his hair never combed until 5pm, growing headier and headier in the armpits, smoking his little Camels, fixing his brandies and soda, padding around with faltering old man's steps, talking in torrential gusts.

By this time Kerouac was drinking more than a quart of brandy and assorted chasers a day. The brandy stimulated him to a point where even barbiturates like Nembutal did not slow him down. Kerouac had once boasted, in a journal entry written in August 1949, that he would "never give up, and that I'll die yelling and laughing," and this vociferous, rowdy energy was still present during Kerouac's last years.

He was still yelling on the visit to Holmes, but on some level he had surrendered, succumbed to what Joyce Johnson called "his vulnerability to profound loneliness and nearly suicidal despair" in her *Washington Post* review of his *Selected Letters: 1940-1956*. Way down deep, Holmes asserted in his journal account of Kerouac's visit, Kerouac wanted to die, "and no amount of self-abuse, disaster or sadness can expunge the feeling of loss and estrangement which has always scarred him." Such people, Holmes observed, leave a permanent mark.

For what seem totemistic reasons, we are fascinated by the alcoholism of modern writers, as if we were surprised that the personal and political disasters Hemingway, Faulkner, or Fitzgerald witnessed should have driven sensitive souls to temper their sorrows with alcohol. Johnson reminded me that Kerouac was a gifted mimic with a photographic memory, even to the point where he could reproduce entire conversations long after they had taken place. Holmes told me in 1982 that anyone who could remember as much as Kerouac could – he called himself "Memory Babe" – would have to find a way to relieve himself of the burden.

But the "burden" was not merely a function of memory. While psychoanalytic terms offer at best only rough categories for human behavior, Kerouac had what some might today call a bipolar personality. This bipolarity formed the central tensions in his work as well as his outlook on his own life and the future of his country, just as it exists in the two great polar regions of our planet. In a journal entry written as a young man of twenty-five on New Year's Day, 1948, he observed that he had read the manuscript of his first novel, *The Town and The City*, and his opinion of it was similar to his opinion of himself: "gleeful and affectionate one day, black with disgust the next." The words suggest the optimism and brooding despair, the desperation to dance before the doom on the horizons that form the north and south poles of his fiction.

A little more than a decade later, in some kind of Dorian Gray reflex, Kerouac's deterioration became evident. Photographs taken in the 1960s document the way Kerouac's Montgomery Clift movie-star look of bruised vulnerability and dark intensity had become bloated into a Balzacian balloon – a distended, unbroken belly beginning in his upper chest, blurred features, huge jowls, and a fog in his eyes. This was the period of late-night desperate calls to former friends all over the country, full of paranoid and delusional remarks.

The publisher Barney Rosset told me that when Kerouac

was living in Northport, Long Island, in the mid-1960s, he would call him railing ferociously about the Jewish New York publishers who would no longer give him a chance. The grotesque awkwardness was emphasized by a ranting vehemence of poisoned feeling, a terrible jeering turbulence evident in one of his last public appearances – the William Buckley television program *Firing Line*. Kerouac was hopelessly drunk in full view of millions of television viewers, helpless in the vise of a sudden celebrity that had flattened him like an oak in an avalanche, and had forgotten him almost as quickly. No wonder that in a poem he compared fame to a dirty newspaper blowing down Bleecker Street. In all fairness, however, some of the element of diatribe and denunciation in Kerouac's last years is the expression of a fool/jerk role that both he and Allen Ginsberg had assumed as a sort of protective disguise in the 1960s when they both began to be so celebrated.

Any "role" or persona, however, can shape personality. The novelist Russell Banks, in an interview in *The Paris Review*, remembered a visit Kerouac made a year before his death. Kerouac appeared with a troupe of some forty followers he had collected in a bar, among them three Micmac Indians from Quebec, who were driving him to Florida to join his mother. Kerouac had received an advance for what would be his last novel, *Vanity of Dulouz*, and was spending it "like a sailor on leave." Kerouac "brought with him a disruptiveness and wild disorder, and moments of brilliance, too," Banks recalled, and could switch personas at will. He could rant one moment and could then offer twenty-minute recitations of William Blake or Hoagy Carmichael song lyrics. For Banks, the rough personalism and expansiveness in Kerouac's work were still present in the man, even though a tortured sadness was dominant.

Like Scott Fitzgerald's, this was one of the saddest American stories. Fitzgerald could not control his drinking, and also died before he was fifty. The saddest element in Kerouac's story was his obstinate denial of the paternity of his daughter, Jan, who had been conceived in 1951 by Joan Haverty, Kerouac's second wife, after the marathon spurt that resulted in *On the Road.* Joyce Johnson, in her exquisite memoir *Minor Characters*, remembers how in 1957 Kerouac had taken a photograph of Jan out of his wallet, arguing that Joan had been sleeping with other men while they were together, and that he was certain he was not Jan's father.

Was Kerouac valuing his literary creation more than the human? Was this an illustration of an artistic irresponsibility that gives some creative souls the space in which to do their work in the first place? If so, how come Kerouac could never separate himself from the mother to whom he was so hopelessly, and perhaps in a figurative sense umbilically, attached.

Joyce Johnson noticed an unmistakable resemblance – a saturnine intensity in the eyes, perhaps? – and that Kerouac had carefully replaced the photograph in his wallet. For Johnson it was not a simple question of "wrong and blame, but of terrible loss and sorrow." That loss and sorrow, however, seems so central in Kerouac's story, and the affirmations of so many of his emboldened characters seem a wilful compensation for it. And on another level, the denial and ultimate abandonment of Jan seem to confirm Burroughs' shrewd observation that Kerouac was "an expert in unconscious sabotage."

There is little question that at the end of his life Kerouac was merely the shell of the man he'd been when he did his best writing. Jan Kerouac wrote an account of her second and final visit to her father in November, 1967, in Lowell. Only fifteen, pregnant, bruised and battered by her promiscuous use of drugs like LSD and heroin, and on her way to Mexico with her boyfriend, she was in some ways a caricature of the excess and restless questing of so many of Kerouac's characters. He sat in a rocking chair with a fifth of whiskey, a foot away from a television watching *The Beverly Hillbillies,* and could barely look at her.

But life is a series of passages. We change as we age, some of us evolve, others devolve and disintegrate. At this point Kerouac was ruined, a different person from the man who once discovered the power and beauty of America in a fast car driven by Neal Cassady. To judge his life, or especially what he had written as a young novelist in his prime, by the standards of what he said in his final decade of despair seems fraudulently unfair, an ironic deployment of the sort of facile moralizing Kerouac excluded from the best of his fiction.

ii.
Burroughs

An Interview with William S. Burroughs

John Tytell: In 1950 you were studying in Mexico City College. What kind of school was that?

William Burroughs: It was organized for people on the G.I. Bill and classes were in English. I studied archeology, mostly Mexican, and Mayan and Aztec. Aztec is very difficult, Mayan very easy.

JT: Where did you do your undergraduate work?

WB: 1936. Harvard. English lit.

JT: Did you take any courses in modern literature?

WB: Not formally.

JT: Did you read Joyce or Eliot then?

WB: Eliot was there as a visiting professor. I went to one of his lectures. He gave lectures and seminars. Eliot was very much something that people were into at that time.

JT: What modern writers most moved you at that time?

WB: I wasn't really in modern literature, but Eliot, Joyce, Kafka, Fitzgerald, of course.

JT: They are making a movie of *The Great Gatsby*.

WB: I'm sure it will be a real mess.

JT: But not at the box office.

WB: I'm not even sure of that. Generally speaking they know what they're doing, but they don't always. They will go all out on these spectaculars that don't work at all. I was just looking the book over myself with an idea of making a film, and there just is no film there – everything's in the prose. You take that away and you've got wooden dialogue and creaky action.

JT: The prose does have an elusive quality so that it appears easy, but underneath the surface is that astonishingly intricate imagery and richness. I think you are right, this will just be a stageshow.

WB: It isn't cinematic.

JT: What did you do after you left Harvard? I'd like to establish a chronology.

WB: A year in Europe studying medicine at the University of Vienna. After that I returned to America and studied psychology briefly at Columbia, then back at Harvard doing graduate work in anthropology. Then a year in New York with an advertising agency. In the army briefly, out again, Chicago where I worked as an exterminator, and at various other jobs. Back to New York in 1943. Left in about '46 for Texas, then New Orleans.

JT: When did you leave for Mexico?

WB: 1949. I stayed in Mexico until 1952, South America in 1953, back in New York in 1953. Then I went to Europe, first to Italy and then Tangiers from about 1954 to 1958. Then Paris. Then between Paris and London during the early sixties. In 1964 I was in Tangiers, in 1965 I was here for a year, and from then on mostly in London.

JT: I would like to ask you specific questions about certain of these years. When you were in New York in 1943, where did you live?

WB: Uptown, downtown, all over. Around the Village, Columbia.

JT: I heard that you worked as a bartender.

WB: For about three weeks on Bedford Street.

JT: It was at that time that you first met Kerouac and Ginsberg. Ann Charters says that Dave Kammerer introduced you. Where had you known Kammerer?

WB: St. Louis. We were brought up together. I'd known him all my life.

JT: I heard that when you first visited Kerouac you were interested in learning how to get seaman's papers?

WB: Vaguely. I did get seaman's papers years later but never used them.

JT: I read in your correspondence that you did what might be termed a "lay analysis" or psychoanalysis of Allen Ginsberg. What was that like?

WB: That's true. It was a very sketchy procedure.

JT: Had you been analyzed?

WB: Oh yes. Waste of time and money.

JT: How did Allen take your analysis?

WB: Well, now he was interested – people like to talk about themselves.

JT: At one time did you share an apartment with Edie Parker, Joan Adams, and Jack Kerouac?

WB: Yes. It was a big apartment and I had a room there for about four or five months in '44.

JT: Do you feel that in any way you influenced Kerouac or Ginsberg at that time?

WB: Influenced in what way?

JT: You've written that certain figures leave their impression in terms of speech and language.

WB: Well I should say that Kerouac influenced me much more than I influenced him because I wasn't at all interested in writing at that time, and he was one of several people who told me I should write. The title of *Naked Lunch* was his, not mine.

JT: Kerouac would later type portions of that novel for you in Tangiers.

WB: That was many years later.

JT: I wanted to ask how that book finally came together, and what role others may have had in helping you assemble it.

WB: One of the key figures was Sinclair Beiles who was working for Girodias at that time.[1] Girodias had seen the novel, not the version that finally appeared but a version that I had before. Remember that there were about a thousand pages to this from which the final material was selected, and some

---

1 Maurice Girodias (1919-199), founder of Olympia Press, notable for publishing controversial authors like Burroughs, Henry Miller, and Vladimir Nabokov.

of the overflow went into *The Soft Machine*, *The Ticket That Exploded*, *Nova Express*, and some of it is still unpublished, and in the archives.

JT: Was any of the original material part of *Queer*?

WB: No. That was a separate thing and way back.

JT: Carl Solomon told me of reading it and feeling that it wasn't the right time to bring it out.

WB: Ace had no intention of bringing it out. Wyn said I'd be in jail if it was published. But it has very little to do with subsequent material from which *Naked Lunch* was assembled.

JT: How did you first meet Huncke?

WB: Through Bob Brandenberg who was a sort of marginal hoodlum who used to hang around the West End in 1944.

JT: Huncke told me the story about the morphine syrettes and was it a sawed off shotgun or a pistol?

WB: No, it was a sub-machine gun.

JT: But that's a fairly large weapon.

WB: This guy stole it and carried it out under his coat.

JT: Was it an army weapon?

WB: Yes. He had smuggled this thing out and nobody wanted to touch it. I finally sort of gave it away to somebody.

JT: Could one get ammunition for that?

WB: Sure. Standard .45.

JT: Huncke told me that you maintained an apartment on Henry Street on the Lower East Side then.

WB: That's right. I had that apartment for fifteen dollars a month. A walk-in kitchen and a few small rooms.

JT: How did you start with morphine?

WB: Well the syrettes were the beginning. I met this guy named Phil White who bought some of the syrettes from me, and he turned me onto the morphine. Then I started going around with him to doctors.

JT: Getting script, as you call it in *Junkie*. When had opium become illegal?

WB: Since the Harrison Narcotics Act around 1914. But you could still get preparations like paregoric.

JT: Was Huncke a new kind of person for you to have met, or had you met people like him before.

WB: No, I'd not met anyone like Huncke before.

JT: What attracted you to him?

WB: Well, you know, he had some interesting stories. Also, he was associated with Phil White and we would get junk together.

JT: Didn't Huncke introduce you to Bill Garver?

WB: He did. He had been in jail, and then he brought Garver around to Joan's apartment.

JT: Garver was a notorious coat-thief, wasn't he?

WB: That's true. He also had a small income of twenty-five dollars a week from his father which was not enough for his habit. So he had to supplement that by stealing overcoats. When his father died, he came into about three to four hundred dollars a month. That's when he moved to Mexico. Later we lived in the same building. He is Bill Gains in *Junkie*.

JT: Huncke told me that he introduced you to Dr. Kinsey when Kinsey began his research in Times Square.

WB: He did indeed. Kinsey and Ward Pomeroy. We met at a place called The Angler, which was on Eighth Avenue between 42nd and 43rd.

JT: Did Kinsey interview you?

WB: No, Pomeroy did.

JT: Did you know Bill Cannastra?

WB: I never met him. I heard a lot about him from Allen Ginsberg, but more particularly from Alan Ansen.[2]

JT: I asked you earlier whether you thought you had in any way influenced Ginsberg or Kerouac, and you said that Kerouac had influenced you more, because he made you aware of writing, but Allen Ginsberg told me that one way you definitely influenced both of them was with books that you suggested that they read, that he had no introduction to modern literature and that you gave him Hart Crane and Auden and Eliot and other books, like Kafka, and that you gave Kerouac Spengler.

WB: And perhaps Celine.

JT: Were you reading Wilhelm Reich at the time?

WB: Either then or later.

JT: What about Lucien Carr? Was he part of your circle then?

WB: Yes. I'd known Lucien from St. Louis, introduced to him by David Kammerer. I saw Lucien subsequently in Chicago when I was there.

JT: Did you meet frequently with Kerouac, Ginsberg, Carr, or were your encounters sporadic?

WB: Sporadic. I saw a lot of Dave because I had known him for a long time and he lived right around the corner on Morton Street when I lived in the Village. The others lived uptown, and I saw more of them when I moved there.

JT: When you shared the apartment with Ginsberg, Joan Adams, and Edie Parker?

---

2 Ansen was a poet and playwright who was friends with many Beat figures, and appears frequently as a character in their work.

WB: That's right. Edie Parker who married Jack Kerouac.

JT: After Jack had been apprehended as an accessory to Carr's murder of Kammerer?

WB: Not as an accessory but a material witness.

JT: How did that happen? I've heard so many different versions, and that Kammerer had been Carr's scoutmaster.

WB: There was some such connection. Then they took a trip to Mexico, and there was trouble between Kammerer and Lucien's mother.

JT: I read in your correspondence that you and Kerouac wrote a novel based on the friendship and subsequent murder.

WB: We did write such a novel – *The Hippos Were Boiled In Their Tanks*.

JT: How did you get that title?

WB: It was in a news broadcast about a circus fire, so we used that.

JT: Is the book in your archives?

WB: No, we can't get hold of it. It's with Sterling Lord.[3] Richard Aaron was supposed to come over here and try and recover it.[4]

JT: What led you to leave New York?

WB: Well, there was a definite likelihood of legal difficulties. When I left I went to Texas.

JT: That's when you began farming?

WB: No, it wasn't. I forgot, I first left, and then I came back to New York, and then left again, so it was two times that I left.

---

3 A literary agent who championed Kerouac and Kesey.

4 Aaron was the publisher of Am Here Books and also helped Burroughs to sell his archives.

JT: Huncke told me that after the New Waverly scene, you, Neal Cassady, and Huncke returned to New York in a jeep from New Waverly.

WB: That was later.

JT: From reading your letters I could tell that you were hassled by bureaucrats at the time you were farming, or at least that you resented their controls a great deal.

WB: Well, there were cotton allotments and all kind of rules. We were ok on that, but not always, and then there was a matter of loans that had to be negotiated. It's really no operation for people who are operating with small capital. If anything goes wrong you're wiped out.

JT: So you're totally at the mercy of credit?

WB: Completely.

JT: In the letters you describe that the relativity of the law had never been clearer to you because of your experience with farming. In particular because of the wetbacks, the way they would be encouraged to come in by the state, and at the same time there could be penalties selectively applied.

WB: Very selectively applied. You got in wrong with the authorities and a truck would drive up and take all your wetbacks away, and you'd be left in cotton picking season with no help.

JT: At the same time, any wetback would be earning five times what he could get in Mexico.

WB: But this didn't happen to the big farmers.

JT: Because they had protection?

WB: Yes. In the big ranches the wetbacks were herded all over the place. They had guards with machine guns. They tried to pull a strike once and the guards shot three of them, so they all went back to work. They had no rights.

JT: In New Waverly you also grew grass. Were you farming anything else?

WB: Couldn't farm anything else.

JT: Was the soil bad?

WB: The problem was how were you going to farm, what with? I mean you could get a horse and plow and do subsistence farming.

JT: Cassady and Ginsberg visited you in New Waverly. What was your impression of Cassady?

WB: I thought he was a very pleasant, easy-going person.

JT: I've heard that he was very intense, capable of long monologues. Was that true then?

WB: I always felt his capacity for silence. I've been with him for eight hours and never exchanged a word.

JT: What kind of driver was he?

WB: Brilliant, a fantastic driver. I had a jeep and the clutch and brakes were out, and he could brake it by putting it into reverse.

JT: I heard that he drove Kesey's bus at high speeds around curves, knowing somehow that there was nothing coming the other way.

WB: He was capable of unbelievable feats of instant calculation.

JT: How did you spend your days in New Waverly? Were you writing at that time?

WB: No, no, no. I didn't write anything, hardly, until I was thirty-five. Anyway I wasn't writing. But there were always things to do, like put a fence around the place, cut wood, walk around.

JT: Was the country beautiful?

WB: It was heavy timber. Oak and persimmon, not too much pine. The kind of country that starts in southern Missouri and goes all the way down to east Texas. There were raccoons and foxes and squirrels and armadillos.

JT: What led you to invite Huncke to the New Waverly place?

WB: I don't remember.

JT: How long was he there?

WB: Quite a while. Four or five months.

JT: Did Kerouac visit you there?

WB: No, he didn't visit.

JT: He visited you on several other occasions, though?

WB: He lived with me in New Orleans, then later in Mexico.

JT: Had he written *The Town and The City* then?

WB: Yes.

JT: Had you seen any of it? Did you know you were a character in it?

WB: I hadn't seen any of it at that time, but he told me I appeared in it.

JT: What was his mood like then?

WB: It was very good.

JT: In one of the letters you mention that on a later visit in Mexico, I think in 1952, he was depressed, uncooperative, and unhappy.

WB: He was moody and a little bit paranoid.

JT: Do you think the difficulty he was having getting *On the Road* accepted had anything to do with this attitude?

WB: Possibly. But then he seemed to take that rather philosophically. The book was literally years kicking around. Malcolm Cowley liked it, but the editor-in-chief didn't at all, and so there were all those delays which might have been just as well because the timing of the book was good. Had it been published earlier, it might not have received the same attention.

JT: That's an interesting point. And he did a lot of writing during the six years between finishing *On the Road* and its publication in 1957.

WB: Oh yes. He was always writing.

JT: Can you tell me more about the history of *Naked Lunch*?

WB: I had this great amorphous manuscript. Girodias had seen some of it and had rejected it. I was in Paris. This was 1958. Allen Ginsberg was also there and he sent selections off to Irving Rosenthal for *The Chicago Review*, and then *The Chicago Review* folded in protest after having difficulty with the university over the issue because of my material and something about Kerouac as well, and then Rosenthal published it in *Big Table*. That was what called it to Girodias' attention. He saw *Big Table* and said, "Now I want the book." So he sent Sinclair Beiles over to my room who said Girodias wants to publish the book, and he wants it done in two weeks. So I got busy, and Brion Gysin helped with typing – Allen had gone – and Sinclair Beiles was most helpful.[5] I was just typing it out and giving it to Beiles with the idea that when we got galley proofs I could decide the final order. But he took one look at it and said, "Leave it the way it is." So it was just really an accidental juxtaposition. And the book was out a month later.

JT: That's a kind of "automatic" structuring – without any wilful control. How does that approach Kerouac's idea of

5 Burroughs had known Gysin in Tangiers, but the two become close friends in Paris, and would remain friends until Gysin's death in 1986; Beiles was a South African poet and editor for Olympia Press.

spontaneity?

WB: Kerouac was not thinking of an accidental procedure but of spontaneity in writing. He was always very opposed to writing with "cut-ups" which is, in a sense, an accidental procedure. Kerouac believed the first version was the best, and I have never found this to be true. I work over things and edit them very carefully.

JT: When Girodias took *Naked Lunch* you were living at the "Beat Hotel," 9 Rue Git le Couer?

WB: And Olympia Press was around the corner. Girodias had inherited the press from his father. It was then called The Dial Press, and they had originally come from Manchester. Girodias' brother later translated *Naked Lunch* into French, and Gallimard took it a year after it had been published in English.

JT: Wasn't there an obscenity trial in the States?

WB: Two. The first one was in Boston where we won on appeal, then in Los Angeles we won in the lower courts. By that time it was pretty well established that there was no censorship on the written word.

JT: Has Henry Miller been a writer who in any way influenced you?

WB: No.

JT: Had you read de Sade?

WB: I looked at de Sade when I was in Paris. Girodias had some translations, but I found it heavy going.

JT: Did you have any interest in Gertrude Stein when you were at Harvard?

WB: I read *Three Lives* there.

JT: Later, did Brion Gysin try to interest you in her work?

WB: No, but he knew her. She was the one who told Paul

Bowles that he shouldn't stay in Paris, but should find some other place.[6]

JT: What were your lodgings like at 9 Rue Git le Couer?

WB: A single room. I had an alcohol stove in the room. There was no phone, but I had red tile floors. It was very cheap.

JT: Judging from letters, Ginsberg, Kerouac, everyone seems to have stayed there.

WB: At different times.

JT: Where was the Villa Delirium?

WB: That was the Muniria in Tangiers where I lived for a number of years.

JT: I read in your letters that when you first went to Tangiers you lived in a whorehouse. What was that like? Faulkner once said in an interview that a whorehouse was the ideal place for a writer to live.

WB: It was not that kind of whorehouse at all. It was just a small place where Tony Dutch, who ran it, rented out rooms. Tony was a great cook and if you wanted to take meals there you could. After that I moved into Muniria where I stayed off and on for many years. It's changed hands many times. First it was owned by a Belgian whose son was involved with smuggling, then it was run by an ex-madam from Inchochina. She had an "in" with the authorities and ran it for many years without trouble. She sold out and a retired British civil servant took it over.

JT: I have some other miscellaneous questions. What about the story that your first wife was a Hungarian countess?

WB: She wasn't. Her name was Ilse Herzfeld Klapper. They were solid, wealthy bourgeois Jewish people in Hamburg.

---

6 Bowles was one of the most famous American expatriate writers, spending fifty-two years in Tangiers. Burroughs' own move to Tangiers had been partly inspired by Bowles' novel, *The Sheltering Sky*.

She had to get out because of Hitler and went to Yugoslavia, and I married her in Athens to get her into the States. She supported herself by working in a travel agency and various jobs. She was very efficient. She was secretary for Ernst Toller, a leftist playwright who tried to commit suicide several times. But he always arranged it so that someone would come and prevent him. And she was a very punctual person. If she went to lunch at twelve she would be back at twelve-thirty. It just so happened that she ran into an old acquaintance in the street and was ten minutes late, and when she returned he was dead in the bathroom. At his funeral she met Kurt Kaszner, a famous Austrian actor who had married a very rich American girl. She became his secretary. Then Mrs. Kuszner died, and the servants said he had poisoned her and she was dug up again, but there was nothing in it. She died of natural causes. Then she worked for John le Touche as his secretary until he died under mysterious circumstances.

JT: I've heard that you had applied to the O.S.S. during the war.

WB: I did and was not accepted. I went down and saw Bill Donovan with a letter of introduction from an uncle, but he referred me to somebody else and nothing happened.

JT: You mentioned that you were in the army.

WB: For a short time, five months. I was stationed in St. Louis.

JT: When was that?

WB: During the war, in 1942 I think.

JT: Do you record your dreams?

WB: I write them down.

JT: How do you do it?

WB: I wake up six times in the course of the average night. I'll just make a few notes. If it's of interest, I transcribe it in the morning. I get at least half, perhaps more, of my material from dreams. Characters, sets, etc.

JT: Can you tell me about the Dutch Schultz filmscript?

WB: I had been interested in Dutch Schultz for a long time, having read his famous last words. There were about 2,000 of them since he was shot on October 23rd at 10pm, and he died about twenty-four hours later, and they had a police stenographer at his bedside. Anyway, he presumably wrote all his words down, though he was delirious and the stenographer may have missed words. Then David Budd came over with quite a bit of research material, that is to say, a series of articles that had appeared in *Colliers* by his lawyer, Dixie Davis.[7] I became interested and wrote a film treatment which was about fifteen pages. This was published in *Harper's*. Then someone named Harrison Starr wanted to produce this as a movie so he paid me a sum of money – ten thousand dollars or something like that – for me to write a film play which I wrote, and that was published by Grollier Press as *The Last Words of Dutch Schultz*. There were other negotiations and I went on to write a full length film script, a shoot script, in 1971.

JT: Wasn't part of *Naked Lunch* written like that, as a film script?

WB: No, in play form, but I'm talking about a shooting script, like indoors, medium shot, or close-up. So that was 195 pages. Richard Seaver is publishing that with a lot of stills. But the film was never made.[8]

JT: How come?

WB: Well, the people were interested, but it was expensive. All gangster films are expensive to make.

---

7 Budd was an abstract painter to whom Burroughs dedicated *The Last Words of Dutch Schultz*.

8 Seaver was an editor for Grove and Viking, and was instrumental in the publication of controversial texts in the fifties and sixties.

JT: Is anyone trying to film *Naked Lunch*?

WB: Brion Gysin did a script, but it seems to be up in the air.

JT: Years ago you said you were writing a Zen western novel about a gunfighter.

WB: I never actually wrote it.

JT: Can you tell me about Kells Elvins?

WB: I met him at the age of twelve at the John Burroughs School. He was at Harvard in 1938 when we wrote the story called "Twilight's Last Gleaming," which was published almost verbatim in *Nova Express*. That story was the beginning of Dr. Benway.

JT: What was the John Burroughs School?

WB: Just a private day school in Clayton, Missouri. We moved out to Clayton which was a suburb of St. Louis. The school was right down the road and Kells lived up the road.

JT: So you knew him since childhood.

WB: And I wrote to him in 1961 saying that the story would appear in *Nova Express* which does mention that he is the co-author, and found out from his mother that he had died about four months before that.

JT: In your last books you seem to be using cut-ups more selectively that previously.

WB: I use them very selectively now. You see *Minutes To Go* was experimental. Now I may make a cut-up of a page and only use a sentence or two.

JT: They seem to be more deliberately used in *The Wild Boys*, and the result is greater impact jarring you into a dream or different reality.

WB: Just cut-up something, and suddenly you'll get a sentence that's right. Like the technology of writing that I'm going into in this course. This sentence came right out of a cut-up: "Technology requires a why." You have to know what you're doing to figure everything out while you're doing it.

JT: That's an odd word choice. Technology rather than technique.

WB: But it's the same thing. Technology or technique – it's a way of doing something.

JT: How do you find teaching at CCNY? Have you taught before?

WB: I just gave two lectures at University of the New World in Switzerland in 1972, I think. I do enjoy teaching at CCNY. I don't know whether my students are learning anything, but I'm learning a great deal, and making my own ideas explicit. I'm considering the question of whether there is a technology for writing as there is for learning to fly, or for learning physics, or engineering. Now how many of those who fly have taken courses in flying, or how many physicists have taken courses in physics – well, obviously all of them – but how many writers have taken courses in writing?

JT: You never took courses in writing.

WB: More haven't than have.

JT: One wonders whether it is a craft that can be taught – I can see how you can be helped by a critic sensitive to your own strengths and weaknesses.

WB: Well, following it right through, taking learning to fly or physics. You're wasting your time unless you meet certain qualifications. If you're going to be a flier you've got to have coordination, a certain degree of intelligence, or you're wasting your time. Given that, these things can be taught. But given all the qualifications for writing, whatever those may be, like some ability to empathize with other people's minds – well a writer like Beckett doesn't need that because he's on his own, going inside, so it may not always apply.

Another factor may be the physical discipline, spending long hours writing. For example, if you are learning something like skiing or karate you have to have an instructor, and if you do it and don't do it right your performance is going to decline. This is not true of writing. Writing is learned by writing. Kerouac, when I first met him, had already written a million words, and that was when he was twenty-three. And lots of it was very bad.

JT: There was this early novel called *The Sea is my Brother*.

WB: He had many different manuscripts, and I read most of it, and thought it was pretty bad. But writers learn from bad writing, but a skier does not learn from bad skiing.

JT: There is a more direct relationship between experience and practical act with writing than most of us imagine. I guess good writers reach a point when they can finally do it, as with Kerouac, when he could become, as it were, spontaneous.

WB: At any rate I've learned about writing and the technology of writing by teaching this course.

JT: Do you plan to write about that?

WB: I'm having all the lectures transcribed. Naturally I have extensive notes, but there's always extemporizing, questions.

JT: Do you have good students?

WB: They are quite a receptive group.

JT: I wanted to tell you that a number of my students seem to be sexually excited by a book like *The Wild Boys*, especially by the association of violence and sexuality. Even in *Naked Lunch* they admit to being turned on despite the elements of comedy or parody.

WB: I find that sexual passages are the most difficult to write. I don't mean the pornographic novels, the ones Girodias was publishing, because they're not sexy at all. They're very easy to write. People write them as fast as they can type. That pornographic style derives from *Fanny Hill*, which is about as unsexy as you *can get.* Actually, most of those books are written by junkies, and they have no sexual feeling about what they are writing.

JT: There are sections of your work that play with pornographic situations very successfully, like "Seeing Red" in *The Wild Boys* where a man comes through customs with a dirty picture that is left undescribed but which causes paroxysms for the officials.

WB: I think description of any sort is difficult, but sexual passages have to be written and rewritten.

JT: Does this have to do with a basic repression we all have, a fear to describe sex?

WB: No, it's just as hard to describe anything. Straight narrative is easy. If I attend to a narrative I can write it almost as fast as I can type.

JT: There seems to be a return to narrative elements in your recent books, *The Wild Boys* and *Exterminator!* You seem to be using experimental devices more sparingly.

WB: With more deliberate intent, I think.

JT: Could you define obscenity in literature?

WB: I don't think it means anything. What they mean is explicit sex scenes, but that's all soft-core now. There's virtually no censorship left on the written word. Where it might occur is if you have something out of the hard-core circuit. There has been some trouble with "Last Tango."

JT: If that's true, will shame and fear be less an agency of control in this society?

WB: Undoubtedly. But of course it is confined to certain areas. I think a very healthy degree of liberation has occurred. You read the Presidential Report in which they just said that

50% of people who saw sex on film found that they were sexually freer. Just the impact of seeing people doing these things on the screen makes people realize, "Well, why in the hell should anyone worry about it?" If the actor is willing to get up there without any mask on, how can you be ashamed of it?

JT: Michael McClure wrote that his intention was "to free the word fuck of its chains."[9] Has that happened?

WB: It has: there are no chains there.

JT: And no future possibility of chains?

WB: I doubt it, unless something drastic happens.

JT: You seem, more than most writers, to have been occupied with kinds of scientific inquiry, and this is reflected in your story situations, for example the character in *The Wild Boys* who stores electricity during shock therapy and then releases it through his eyes as a death ray. At the same time, I don't feel that you can be seen as a science fiction writer.

WB: I've talked to a lot of science fiction writers about this. The younger and more progressive ones maintain that the old categories are breaking down, and science fact has overtaken science fiction. In books like *The Terminal Man* the subject is not what's going to happen in three hundred years, but things that can have been done right now. So the ideas about science fiction are changing as science overtakes it.

JT: Do you read science fiction?

WB: When I have time, but only when I can find any that's good. I'll get a stack and most of it is terrible though there are some good ideas. But there are very few that can convince you that it ever could have happened anywhere.

JT: Have you read anything by Rudolph Wurlitzer?

---

9 McClure is a Beat poet who read with Ginsberg at the Six Gallery Reading in 1956.

WB: I read *Nog* and liked it.

JT: What about someone like Robbe-Grillet?

WB: Haven't read him. I saw an excellent movie based on his work.

JT: What about Beckett?

WB: Well, yes. I would think of Beckett in the same way as Genet, as a writer that I admire very much.[10] I've read practically everything Genet has written. He's a very great writer and not writing anymore.

JT: You met him in Chicago, didn't you, in 1968?

WB: Genet said there were two things: me and the French language. I've put one into the other et c'est faites. With Beckett I like the early novels best, like *Watt* and *Malone Dies*. Now he's getting too hermetic.

JT: Rather than simply informing us of a vision of the future, as in *The Wild Boys*, I feel the ultimate end of your fiction is a kind of alchemy – magic based on precise and incantatory arrangement of language to create particular effects, such as the violation of western conditioning.

WB: I would say that was accurate, but I would also say that I am creating a character. And my characters are always a composite: Say I have a dream of a character that looks like this, then I'll find a picture or a person, and then maybe a character in someone else's story. One tries to create a vision of a living being. Of course the beginning of writing – after all, remember that the written word is an image; we forget this but we don't have a pictorial writing but the written word is an image and painting and writing were originally one and the same. The purpose of those paintings was magical, that is to produce the effect that is depicted.

JT: Is your intention shamanistic, to ward off disaster?

---

10 Jean Genet (1910-1986), controversial French novelist and poet.

WB: Not necessarily disaster, but certainly to produce effects. For example, all primitive sculpture is magical, but as soon as these things are sold to tourists they have no vitality. The saying is that painting, writing, and sculpture are traditionally magic, and that it is intended to produce certain effects.

JT: Like the sense of transformation implicit in the rate of change in all your writing?

WB: There is also the question of the actual relations between formal ritual magic and writing. People who are into ritual magic like Aleister Crowley – he may have been a competent black magician but he is not a good writer. In fact, he's not readable.

JT: Have you studied magic formally or involved yourself in any kind of cult systems?

WB: Well ,the whole content of the Mayan books is obviously magical, but we can't understand very much of it because Bishop Landa burned so much of the writing.

JT: Have you studied any other non-Western procedural maps like *The Book of the Dead*? Or gnostic texts like the *Cabala*?

WB: Not very deeply. I've looked at *The Book of the Dead.* I've read a lot of the literature of magic, but never involved myself very deeply.

JT: Is there any practical accommodation of magic in your work as a writer?

WB: Well, I simply feel that all magic *is* magic. That is if you get a very subtle evocation of the 1920s in Fitzgerald…

JT: Yes. But that's "magic" in a romantic sense, the idea of evoking a memory onto a page and while that's beautiful, I was thinking of weaving a spell.

WB: But "weaving a spell" is magic. Now you've got the kind of magic that newspapers are involved in, people like

Luce who were quite consciously capable of creating events. There is a very definite technique for doing that, and some of it is very much like magic – they stick someone full of pins and then show the picture to millions of people and they will get an effect. Do you realize to what extent being on the front cover of *Time* is a kiss of death? The Nobel Prize is another one. Hearst used to say that he didn't write the news, he made it. But that is all negative magic which has very little to do with the writer's work.

Hello, Mr Nice Guy

"Nothing is true, everything is permitted."
- Hassan ibn Sabbah

I – The Majoon Prophet

William Burroughs was unimpressed by fame and did his best to avoid its consequences. He had written, in *Naked Lunch*, a landmark of postmodernism that had begun as letters to his friend Allen Ginsberg. Writing in Tangiers under the influence of heavy opiates and majoon, a hashish confection, he described his fantasies, debilitations, and terrors of addiction from the inside. This was an audacious subject matter in the 1950s, but even more important was his startling departure in form. He had written an antinovel juxtaposing a series of mordantly bizarre burlesque sketches – he called them "routines" – all fragmented, discontinuous, expressing a hallucinated conspiratorial vision with surreal hyperbole.

Burroughs predicted our catastrophic national appetite for drugs. In 1947, he attempted to grow opium on a ninety acre spread he had purchased in East Texas, a bayou area with pine woods, low rolling hills, and weather-beaten farmhouses. Opium does not grow north of the Rio Grande, but secreted between rows of alfalfa, Burroughs grew a crop of poor-quality marijuana. With Neal Cassady at the wheel of an old jeep, Burroughs drove to Times Square and sold it, anticipating a contraband business worth fortunes today in states like Georgia, Arkansas, and Hawaii.

In a series of fictions drawn from life through a prism of paranoia, he revealed our unlimited capacity for violence and the repercussive dangers of police surveillance and state control. He was, in short, an American Orwell, though like Tiresias, whom the gods installed in a bordello with the attributes of both sexes, he had to suffer to attain his vision.

II – The Ugly Spirit

I met Burroughs in the spring of 1973. The writer, known as "El Hombre Invisible" had recently returned to this country after more than two decades of self-imposed exile in Tangiers and Europe. He was living in what he called "The Bunker" – a cavernous, windowless, former YMCA locker room on the Manhattan Bowery, the street of derelicts and dead dreams.

I had published an essay full of praise for *Naked Lunch.* Although by reputation Burroughs was supposed to be glacial, I wanted to interview him for the book I was writing on the Beats, and I was nervous about it. I surmised, from reading a letter written to Allen Ginsberg in 1952, that Burroughs could be hostile: "I never swallowed the other cheek routine, and I hate the stupid bastards who won't mind their own business. I like very few people, as a matter of fact, and what happens to people I don't like, like the song says ''tis their misfortune and none of my own.'"

Burroughs sat at the end of a long metallic table. He was diffident, punctiliously self-contained, and cool as a knife blade. He stared right past me into a middle distance, and he had little patience for small talk.

I felt a crusty brittleness. It might have been a residual class affectation that reminded me of T.S. Eliot, and he told me he had seen Eliot read while he was in residence at Harvard when Burroughs was an undergraduate there. Burroughs was wearing mortuary colors: a black shirt, no tie, a three-button wool vest, and matching black trousers. It resembled the banker's look I remembered from photos of Eliot, but it seemed curiously out of place, a disguise of sorts. My unease was furthered by a dry irritated edge to his tone; he kept punctuating my queries with an impatient: "Next!"

To my consternation, Burroughs insisted that because of stylistic differences he should not be identified with the Beat movement. American writers despise classification and category. I realize that Hemingway or Fitzgerald would have offered similar disclaimers had they been associated with the Lost Generation. Burroughs was an iconoclast, an extreme individualist who lacked the qualities of sympathy so prevalent in almost all the other Beats, but the evidence of his participation in Beat history was overwhelming.

As a group, writers tend to be competitive and independent. In 1944, as a sign of the unusually close kinship of the Beats, Burroughs shared a large communal apartment with Kerouac, Ginsberg, and several women. Burroughs would use Kerouac as a sort of conduit to Ginsberg, who later became his agent and, for a brief space, his lover. In 1944, Burroughs collaborated with Kerouac on an unpublished novel called *And the Hippos were Boiled in their Tanks*. Impressed by his ability as a raconteur, Kerouac predicted that Burroughs would one day write a novel called *Naked Lunch*, and over a decade later, in Tangiers, he would help type it.

I knew that Burroughs was colder, more cunning and calculating, than Kerouac. After all, he had once declared that love was a "fraud perpetrated by the female sex," a notion Kerouac, by inclination always more of a romantic, would never accept. Burroughs was the factualist who represented an uncompromising truth, even to the point of hurtfulness.

When he met Kerouac in 1944 he surmised – quite correctly, as it turned out – that Kerouac was so emotionally bound to his mother that he would never be able to leave her side either physically or spiritually. In a letter to Ginsberg written in July 1958 he suggested, with one of his brilliant medical images, that Kerouac had been "sewed up like an incision" by his mother, a woman Burroughs categorically dismissed as "a stupid, small-minded vindictive peasant."

A man seemingly devoid of sentiment, Burroughs was much less interested in the past than in the present, and I recalled that in the "Atrophied Preface" at the end of his masterpiece, *Naked Lunch*, he had suggested that he was trying to write without memory. An intention of such immediacy is rare among writers. Burroughs acknowledged that he did not share Kerouac's interest in spontaneity, although in an undergraduate course at Harvard he had been fascinated by Coleridge's use of opium as a means of facilitating a writer's flow.

Mustering all my courage, I asked him to describe the circumstances of his fatal shooting of his common-law wife, Joan Vollmer Adams, in Mexico City in 1951. I knew this disastrous event was a personal fulcrum for Burroughs, the wound that finally precipitated his art. He had been a blocked writer for years, but at the age of thirty-seven, during his trial, he wrote his first books, *Junkie* and *Queer*, a book published much later. Burroughs winced, then mumbled a reply while moving out of range of my tape recorder. I practically had to read his lips. It was an enormously uncomfortable moment for both of us.

When *Naked Angels* was published in 1976, Burroughs

complained about my portrait of him, which he felt exaggerated his family's money and connections. He claimed I had been seduced by Kerouac's mythmaking, although I knew about a letter he had sent Kerouac from Tangiers in September, 1954, that mentioned the "St. Louis Country Club set" in which he had been raised. Ginsberg had confirmed this perspective in interviews with me, and it is clear that both Ginsberg and particularly Kerouac, with his lower-working-class background, saw Burroughs as affluent.

In *Naked Angels*, I wrote that I thought Burroughs had the "hauteur of an aristocrat who has known the gutter," which was the impression he gave me when we met. I had never mentioned the fact that his parents were listed in the St. Louis Social Register, and that his mother's brother, Ivy Lee, who owned a townhouse just off Fifth Avenue and who had been John D. Rockefeller's publicist, was listed in the New York Social Register. His daughter Alice, Burroughs' first cousin, had been presented in London at the court of St. James. If that wasn't a social connection, what was?

Burroughs' grandfather was a Princeton graduate who had perfected the adding machine by incorporating an oil cylinder. He dissipated much of the money he received from the Burroughs Corporation before dying young from tuberculosis and alcoholism. But Burroughs and his older brother attended private schools, his family moved to a big house situated on a five acre lot when he was ten, and his parents had a summer house where they employed a maid, a butler, a nanny, a cook, and a gardener. When Burroughs was fifteen, in 1929, his parents took their two sons to France for a grand tour in a chauffeured car. His father had the good sense to sell a quarter of a million dollars' worth of Burroughs stock just before the Depression, so both boys could attend Harvard during its depths and receive an allowance long beyond graduation.

Of course, no one in the Burroughs clan ever was as wealthy as the Rockefellers. Like F. Scott Fitzgerald, Burroughs was *haute bourgeoisie*, on the fringes of the very rich, attending the same schools but invited only to the larger parties, while at the same time snubbed for never having quite enough money. His best friend and neighbor in St. Louis, Kells Elvins, was the son of a former congressman who was born in a town in Missouri named after his family, but Burroughs' mother ran a shop. Although he was raised in privileged circumstances, his exclusion from the inner circles of the very wealthy – which he regarded as a sort of primal disinheritance – gave him a crucial ambivalence about class and money.

What is interesting about Burroughs' reaction to the biographical portrait I offered in *Naked Angels* was his overreaction, and the myth of himself on which he insisted. It reminded me of Henry Miller's belligerent assertion that the protagonist he had imagined in his novels was literally autobiographical. In fact, as his friend Michael Frankel observed, Miller habitually distorted everything. Miller, for example, would tell the story of how his first mother-in-law had seduced him while she was bathing, a perfect fantasy of violated taboos for his fiction, but hardly what happened.

Burroughs chose for himself as the writer's capital the mantle of the heretical outsider formerly assumed by Ezra Pound – the invective in "Canto XIV," Pound's famous attack on British culture, should be seen as one source of Burroughs' rage.

On some level, Burroughs refashioned elements of his background to fit the myth that served him so well. Very early in life, he developed an intense self-loathing, which may be traced to his Welsh nanny. Like Miss Jessel in Henry James' *The Turn of the Screw*, she probably initiated him into sexual improprieties that no child should witness. His sense of himself as peculiar may have been intensified by another family servant, an old Irish cook who believed in the occult, concocted witchlike spells, and taught him the repulsive sorcery of emitting a high-pitched sound that could attract toads.

Like Kerouac and Ginsberg, and, for that matter, both

Pound and Miller, Burroughs had a problem accepting his mother. It drove him to a psychiatrist after he was quickly discharged from the army during the Second World War. Throughout his life he experimented with various eccentric therapies, from Reich's orgone box to L. Ron Hubbard's Scientology, probing the personal consequences of a dominating mother and a reticent, ineffectual father. Burroughs said that his mother had been "crippled by her Bible-belt upbringing" and decided that she projected a "tremulous look of doom and sadness," which is a poetic was of saying she was a terribly depressed person. Laura Lee Burroughs was frequently ill, and Burroughs claimed she was psychic. In her gift shop in St. Louis and later with an antique business in West Palm Beach, she served women who were even wealthier than she was. She also composed three books on floral design for Coca-Cola, in an ironic sense providing the writer-model her son would one day emulate.

Burroughs saw himself as a misfit, a detestable creep, an unwholesome child, "a walking corpse" as he described himself in a repeated anecdote, so any hint of glamour or good fortune contradicted his self-made image as the marginal man, the Outsider, even the pariah like Tiresias. Alone among his peers as an undergraduate at Harvard, he kept a pistol in his drawer and a ferret as a pet, discouraging visitors.

When he shot Joan Vollmer in Mexico City he was suffering from what he described in *Queer* as a nightmarish depression. He claimed he was seized by a recurrent "ugly spirit" with which he would always struggle. In a letter to Ginsberg, dated March 18th, 1949, a year before the shooting, Burroughs wrote that his relationship to Joan was from the beginning at an impasse and "not amenable to any solution."

In *On the Road* Kerouac offers a tight glimpse of Burroughs e*n famille* when Sal visits Joan Vollmer and Burroughs, Old Bull Lee in the novel, in New Orleans. The scene is based on a visit Kerouac made in 1949. Kerouac comments on the strangeness of the relationship with Joan, which Burroughs dominated with a dreary, monotonous monologue. Kerouac, always too generous depicting his pals, decided Joan's attachment to Burroughs was "delirious," resulting in an unfathomably "deep companionship," and what seemed like "curiously unsympathetic and cold between them was really a form of humor."

In the scene, Kerouac also catches Burroughs' fixation with guns as he shows Sal his arsenal and boasts about a German gun that fired a gas shell capable of killing a hundred men. A practicing marksman, Burroughs always used weapons. He confessed to Ginsberg that the "William Tell act" – asking Joan to balance a glass on her head so that he could shoot it off – had been his idea. When the Mexican police arrived, his unbelievable story was that the loaded gun had fallen off the refrigerator when its door had been slammed during an all-night party.

In a letter written several years after the shooting, sent from Tangiers in February, 1955, he speculated that it was as if Joan's "brain *drew* the bullet toward it." Later, in what I regarded as a romantic rationalization, Ginsberg supported this view, telling me he thought Joan was "asking to be suicided" out of a relationship that was no longer tenable.

I have never forgotten a glimpse of the "ugly spirit" I discovered in the Ginsberg Deposit at Columbia University when I was doing the research for *Naked Angels*. A self-portrait by Burroughs done in charcoal with two large black circles for eyes, with calligraphic marks emanating from a black hole of a mouth, it looked as if Kafka's Joseph K had drawn it in an anguish of uncertainty, or in fits of pain. Spectral, haunting, the drawing was a Rorchach test containing all the expressionist horror of Kokoschka, the ominous eeriness of Francis Bacon, the silently savage no-exit warning to stay away of Munch's *The Scream*. This was a man like Conrad's Kurtz, who had seen "the horror, the horror," and didn't particularly want to gossip about it.

III – The Burroughs Cult

I saw Burroughs on a few other occasions in the early 1970s, at a reading at the West End Bar near Columbia University, where the Beat writers used to drink, and in 1973 while auditing a creative writing class he was teaching in place of Kurt Vonnegut at City College.

Burroughs felt that creativity could never be taught. Writing was learned by writing, provided the writer had certain requisite talents. For him, creative writing courses were just a faddish university scam. They were primarily useful as employment for writers who might otherwise be waiting tables, driving taxis, or fabricating jingles in advertising agencies if they were sufficiently gifted, as Burroughs had done for a time years earlier.

In class he was quite formal, always reserved, and only occasionally sardonic as he entertained himself with some observation that was often lost on his students. I heard no whisper of any of the maniacal characters he had invented. Instead he seemed like a decorous grandfather, though one burdened by some worry or terrible strain. The gentility seemed part of another disguise, a self-effacement that permitted him the novelist's role as observer. His students were disappointed, he surmised in an interview, because he wore a coat and tie to class, as if they "had expected me to appear stark naked with a strap-on, I presume."

The question he addressed was whether there was a "technology" for writing, as there was for physics or engineering. Dogmatically, he preferred the word "technology" to "technique," its more humanist cousin. In his world, I sensed, it was better to use his vocabulary.

Once, when a student asked him about the postmodernist sacrifice of clarity and the consequent dangers of incoherence, Burroughs' reply seemed drawn from what he had stated in *The Job* – a collection of interviews about the craft of writing. Things didn't happen in a logical sequence in life, and "any writer who hopes to approximate what actually occurs in the mind and body of his characters cannot confine himself to such an arbitrary structure as 'logical sequence.'"

He dominated the classes I audited with an old-fashioned lecture method, reading from carefully prepared notes that were more expositional than pragmatically connected to text. For a man who professed to despise intellectuals, he seemed very involved in theoretical possibilities for fiction – e.g. the cinematic way to present a story as opposed to one that depended on old-fashioned omniscience.

Heading from Allen Ginsberg that Burroughs needed money, I invited him to read at Queens College. At dinner, he drank vodka and coke, looked down at his food glumly, and barely spoke a word. Before the reading, in a stairwell, he insisted on lighting a joint, which he shared with two pale, thin young men whom he had brought along as a sort of straggling entourage. I must admit that that action made me, as an untenured member of the faculty, extremely nervous.

The reading was held on the top floor of the Student Union, which could accommodate around eight hundred students. Even with little publicity, the room was filled twenty minutes before the reading. When I scanned the crowd, I noticed a brooding element of pre-punk minimalism in the audience, sallow types and older black leather bikers who had heard through some esoteric grapevine that Burroughs was making an appearance.

I had asked him to read "Roosevelt After Inauguration," one of his more outrageous Rabelesian parodies in which the presidential cabinet offices are awarded to pimps, hookers, and thieves, and in which Burroughs imagines acts of copulation between a purple-assed baboon and some of Roosevelt's Supreme Court justices. Burroughs' delivery was crisp and his timing was electrifying, but I was apprehensive about how the bitter parody of his message would be received. At that time, the borough of Queens was still quite conservative. Through the 1960s, the effort in Vietnam had been patriotically supported in Queens, and Burroughs' more jaundiced views surely were suspect in such a place.

I saw him read again in the fall of 1978 at the Nova Convention. Organized on the Lower East Side, the three-day festival featured punk-rock musicians, Keith Richards (who failed to show), performance artist Laurie Anderson, and Patti Smith in a fur coat and iguana boots (but her bronchitis prevented her from singing).

Paul Bowles once remarked that the Burroughs legend existed in spite of Burroughs and not because he sought to pursue it. The most obscure member of the Beat group had suddenly been launched as a cult figure. In the 1970s he appeared as a cool cipher in the crowd on the cover of the Beatles' *Sgt. Pepper's Lonely Hearts Club Band* and was photographed by Andy Warhol, Richard Avedon, Robert Mapplethorpe, and the conceptual artist Les Levine. These manifestations of the Burroughs legend continued through the 1980s when he posed for a series of ads for Nike and the Gap, and played a priest in a role that seemed written just for him in Gus Van Sant's film, *Drugstore Cowboy*.

At the Nova Convention the word was that Burroughs – one of the few to break the most powerful habits of all – was back on heroin. He looked confused, gaunt, and frail. In the spotlight, his skin had a ghostly translucence. It was the first appearance of the "scarecrow suspended from a coat hanger" that James Wolcott would later commemorate in *The New Yorker*.

Led by acolytes to the front of a rowdy standing-room-only crowd, Burroughs was being figuratively crowned by countercultural worshipers, many of whom were unable to concentrate long enough to read his complicated prose. They seemed to revel with him as an icon in the way they might have with a David Bowie or a Lou Reed – two singers who were clearly influenced by him. I wondered whether I was the sole member of that audience who was disturbed by the fact that Burroughs slurred frequently as he read.

IV – All Supermarkets Look Alike

I did not see Burroughs again until the Kerouac Convention celebrating the twenty-fifth anniversary of the publication of *On the Road* in Boulder in 1982. Conducting a series of interviews for a film on Kerouac, I met him at the opening of an art show featuring Kerouac's paintings. When I asked him about them he compared their rough uninformed power to Van Gogh.

The room was full of undergraduates in short skirts swirling around with trays of hors d'oeuvres and martinis. Burroughs was quite drunk. Weaving and balanced by a cane that seemed in his hands like formidable weapon, he was full of a manic, almost diabolic glee that I would see again when he performed one of his characters, Dr. Benway, with a grinning skeletal malice for Howard Brookner's documentary film on Burroughs.

That performance was a moment that seems more threatening in the post-AIDS era. In *Naked Lunch*, Benway is presented as an expert in mind control. As a surgeon he represents authority, and in Burroughs' world such figures usually abuse their authority or sell it to the highest bidder. In a scene of hilariously grotesque pandemonium, Brookner showed Benway botching an open-heart surgery by using a toilet plunger to massage the heart. As a result, copious amounts of blood splattered all over Benway's smock, the anesthesiologist, and the nurse (played by Candy Darling, a transvestite who had been featured in some of Andy Warhol's films). All the way through, like some skinny version of W.C. Fields, Burroughs performed with a deadpan, snarling rancor, his voice an arrogant sneer full of caustic impatience and rage.

Burroughs told me something else at the Boulder art opening that I found startling. He had moved from the Bunker to Lawrence, Kansas, because of his friendship with James Grauerholz, a tall, handsome young man who was his secretary and companion. I asked him whether the move from the East Coast to the plains in the middle of the country had any effect on his imagination. His answer had the impact of a blunt weapon hitting a soft object. With a devastating flatness that discouraged any further inquires on my part, he replied, "To us lone cats, all supermarkets look alike."

I believe in distinctions and articulating differences when they exist, and at first I found his answer more puzzling than accurate. In Boulder, I had seen for the first time an enormous liquor supermarket bathed in what seemed like a million watts of fluorescence. So all supermarkets did not seem alike. Later, I realized that Burroughs' remark came from a man who inhabited an interior space that ultimately was all that he found interesting.

Burroughs was reluctant to be interviewed for my film, but when Ginsberg agreed, and after a lot of negotiation with Grauerholz, he consented. On camera, he was terse and perturbed. I knew that there had been an undeclared rivalry with Kerouac, who represented the heart and who had once accused Burroughs of being all mind. Burroughs kept looking sideways and twitching, body language that told me he could not wait for the interview to terminate.

V – A Stick of Dynamite

One of the aborted interviews I attempted for the Kerouac film in Boulder was with a minor Beat poet named Ray Bremser. I remember a photograph of Bremser by Burt Glinn, part of a piece Kerouac published in a slick magazine called *Holiday* in October, 1959. Bremser is standing in the middle of the Gaslight, a coffeehouse on MacDougal Street in the honky-tonk part of the Village, reading poems to an intent audience. Even though a couple of his auditors are wearing sunglasses, Bremser seems uncertain and curiously out of place.

A rangy, hawkish man, Bremser had been incarcerated for armed robbery at the age of eighteen and had written much of his first book, *Poems of Madness*, in a cell. Bremser wrote a second book of poems, *Angel*, on light brown toilet paper in another jail cell. In Veracruz, Mexico, fleeing a court appearance, he encouraged his wife, Bonnie, to support him and their infant daughter with prostitution, a story she tells with graphic pain in her memoir, *For Love of Ray*.

Bremser had been a drinking buddy of Kerouac's, and like Neal Cassady and Gregory Corso, he epitomized the fast-talking, rollicking, street-hipster, con-man reckless abandon Kerouac romanticized with his glorious roman candle image for madness early on in *On the Road*. Ginsberg, taking this even one romantic step further, saw madness in "Howl" as insurgence of natural ecstasy rather than as the pain suffered by his mother, Naomi.

Bremser was especially edgy and surly, full of a coiling tension I found weird. He didn't quite know why he was talking to me and sized me up as if I were an FBI informant. It was a suspicion I recognized from trying to interview people like Lucien Carr and Herbert Huncke. When Bremser sat down, I noticed a bulge in his glossy high leather boot and asked him about it. Turning almost cheerful, he pulled out a stick of dynamite and explained that western miners provisioned themselves in this manner because they used explosives in their work, and for potential claim jumpers.

Bremser's aura of unpredictable irresponsibility scared me, so I abruptly discontinued the interview. The story is relevant in terms of Burroughs, who represents the dangerous, the less than beatific, side of the Beats. Poets like Ginsberg, Gary Snyder, Philip Whalen, Anne Waldman, Diane di Prima, and Kerouac were serious about Buddhism, but their ability to relate to more incendiary figures like Bremser and Neal Cassady is a sign of the mutual tolerance that helped the Beats cohere.

I suspect Burroughs was the sort of man who might have shouted fire in a crowded theater. What he distrusted most of all was what he would have called the lie of liberalism, which from his libertarian perspective only led to the poison of bureaucracy. "I tell you," he advised Kerouac in 1949, "we are bogged down in this octopus of a bureaucratic socialism." Bureaucrats, he told Kerouac in another letter written a few weeks later, are "a cancer on the political body of this country which no longer belongs to its citizens."

Such sentiments form the thematic argument of *Naked Lunch*. The strongest indictment of what Burroughs saw as the Trojan horse of liberalism occurs in yet another letter to Kerouac written on the first day of 1950:

> Allen [Ginsberg] is aligning himself with a cancerous element that will stifle every vestige of free life in the U.S. You notice that any oppressive, meddling piece of legislation (anti-gun, anti-sex, anti-kick laws) is always loudly supported by the "Liberal" press. The word Liberal has come to stand for the most damnable tyranny, a sniveling, mealy-mouthed tyranny of bureaucrats, social workers, psychiatrists and union officials.

Burroughs once told me that the problem with liberals was that they thought they could legislate evil out of the human character. His fear was based on what he saw as an encroaching police state, although it chillingly anticipates the recent resistance of figures like Timothy McVeigh and far-right, so-called freemen Aryan supremacist groups in the western United States and racist, xenophobic skinheads and hooligans in Europe.

Burroughs and Kerouac too, with the extreme and often inconsiderate individualism of some of the characters in *On the Road* and the alcohol-inspired political views he blurted in his final years, represent a curious conservatism that seems to cut against the grain of the Beat myth, at least as it is popularly conceived. Burroughs particularly is deeply suspicious of a Big Brother state apparatus that invents rules to govern all activities. This is what the Puritans did when they first settled in the northeastern part of America, regulating everything from speech to dress and mandating attendance in church, but they were not able to put a video camera in every room!

VI – Hassan ibn Sabbah

Burroughs is the most extremist of the Beats, because his vision offers no hope. Americans, he believed in his singular fashion, were karmically afflicted and cursed because they had dropped the atomic bomb on Hiroshima.

Burroughs has been our most apocalyptic American writer since Edgar Allan Poe. Marshall McLuhan, reviewing *Naked Lunch* in *The Nation*, observed that criticizing Burroughs was very much like finding fault with the demeanor or dress of the man who was banging on your kitchen door to warn you that your house was on fire. It still seems an apt simile.

Burroughs is our plague artist. The French artist and writer Artonin Artaud proposed that the origin of Greek theater was not in the orgy, as Nietzsche had speculated in *The Birth of Tragedy*, but in a plague that leveled all social distinctions and created a need for rituals of purgation.

Burroughs has a less redemptive view of the unifying possibilities suggested by the plague than Artaud, Kafka, or Camus. The plague state leads to a delirium that is Burroughs' ideal moment, the point at which anything indeed is permitted and nothing seems true, when all distinctions and moral considerations are pointless. Much of Burroughs' fiction anticipates our fears of biological and viral warfare in the twenty-first century, as well as the emphasis on the social controls by the state that are the consequences of such fears.

The plague state is so harrowing because it offers us a historical analogy to the place we imagine as hell. Burroughs consistently explored its recesses from *Naked Lunch* on, and one of his last novels, *Cities of the Red Night*, is full of the exotically turbulent purgatory that for so long characterized his world.

The opening scenes, depicting a death village permeated

by a radioactive virus and a hospital epidemic of sexual delirium, present typical instances of Burroughs' vision, a perspective that sees entropic disease as the correlative to disorder and a breakdown around us. Burroughs brings back for brief appearances certain favorite figures from his former fiction: Dr. Benway, still devoted to germ warfare; Lupita, the junky whore queen of *Naked Lunch*, Captain O'Brian and the Katzenjammer Kids.

Burroughs' characters move in a swirling ambiance of masturbation and ejaculation, of nooses, hangings, and gallows fornication, of astrally projected intercourse and sexual mutilation, of headless men fed through the rectum and used as love slaves, of sex nettles and orchids growing in human flesh, of pouches made of human testicles, of snakes, scorpions, centipedes, and the depraved smiles of idiotic lust appearing everywhere.

Surely the printing press of the future will produce Burroughs' novels complete with the smells and stains of semen galore: "A Firsty Pop is the hyacinth smell of young hard-ons, a whiff of school toilets, locker rooms, and jockstraps, rectal mucus and summer feet, chigger lotion and carbolic soap – whiffs you back to your first jackoff and leaves you sitting there on the toilet –"

Burroughs always gave us sights, sounds, and smells with an insistent clarity, sometimes unsettling his readers with a lurid lyricism. His voice is often laconic and his sentences spare so that the images flash forward all the more brilliantly. These qualities are evident in *Cities of the Red Night* as well as the attempt to relate a story in the juxtaposed fashion of Faulkner's *The Wild Palms*, in which two narratives are played off against each other.

In *Cities of the Red Night*, the first story is set in the eighteenth century as a band of pirates follow some libertarian calling and try to free South America from Spanish oppression. The story is intriguing, involving opium culture and transvestite crews (who entice merchant ships and then overpower them) under the leadership of the effeminate but ruthless Captain Strobe, who develops his revolutionary program in a Conradian setting. Burroughs' theatricality has never been so pronounced (with giant battles and orgies) as Strobe's crew, as various in national origin and ingenuity as Captain Ahab's, rallies to the buccaneer revolution.

Counterpointed to this story is a seamy detective melodrama. Private investigator Clem Snide pursues the trail of a hippie coke dealer who has been decapitated in a brutal sex crime. As readers of Burroughs' fiction know, his characters metamorphose and several voices can exist as aspects of an evolving identity, and so it is no wonder that Burroughs finds ways to join his pirate adventure to Snide's investigations.

Just when Burroughs has us tantalized, halfway through the novel, and without ever resolving either narrative, he introduces the Cities of the Red Night, a group of six fabulous places existing in the Gobi Desert one hundred thousand years ago that destroy one another and the planet in a cataclysmic war. Strobe, Snide, and the other time travelers of Burroughs' fiction participate in this frenzy that involves a CIA plot to exterminate humanity and rebuild it with a white gene pool.

Plot, in Burroughs' hands, is evidently in the service of an imagination that works mythically rather than historically, and his novel is full of parallels to Circe and Pan, to tarot figures, to arcane Egyptian and Mayan magic rituals. In Burroughs' hands such staples of fiction as plot and character are invariably reinterpreted so that critics complain that his characters resemble cartoons more than they do rounded, realizable, even identifiable humans. Such criticism seems quite beside the point, for Burroughs is a postmodernist fabulist, not an imitator of Dickens. And postmodernism, as even so suspicious a historian as Gertrude Himmelfarb has observed (American Scholar, Spring 1997), proposes a radical relativism, a skepticism so absolute as to reject such notions as greatness or even the idea of truth.

For the postmodernist, she alleges, "there is no truth, no knowledge, no objectivity, no reason, and, ultimately, no reality. Nothing is fixed, nothing is permanent, nothing is transcendent… What appears to be real is illusory, deceptive, problematic, indeterminate. What appears to be true is nothing more than what the power structure, the 'hegemonic' authority in society, deems to be true."

Himmelfarb could almost be describing the epistemology governing *Cities of the Red Night*, or the motto of one of its characters, Hassan ibn Sabbah, that because nothing is true, anything is permissible – the nihilistic refrain that appears often as a personal maxim in Burroughs' letters.

An eleventh century Persian religious agitator who founded the Ismaili sect, Hassan ibn Sabbah was known as "the Old Man of the Mountain" because he lived in a fortress located at an altitude of ten thousand feet, near Teheran. As an archetypical terrorist, he trained teams of young assassins who used hashish ritually, and who, in turn, were controlled by Hassan ibn Sabbah through its use. Hassan ibn Sabbah first appears in *Naked Lunch* and reappears as one of Burroughs' prototype code figures, an anarchist from the larger social perspective who used focused control systems to achieve his ends.

Control, irrespective of any relative morality, is the game of the power state. Of course, the "morality" of any time or place is itself the ideological underpinning of any system, the basis for any set of social controls. Manipulation and control were Burroughs' perennial concerns from the time of his studying the Mayan codices in Mexico City in the early 1950s, and Hassan ibn Sabbah and his hashish assassins provide another focus point for Burroughs' fascination with how events can be shaped.

Burroughs interprets Hassan ibn Sabbah's principle as a license for freedom. To the extent that modern life depends on manufactured illusion – achieved through media manipulation and state management – any illusion is feasible and permissible. To arbitrarily and exclusively establish any single view as "real" is to exclude any other possibility.

Burroughs' view is that "morality" never depends on any

innate principle, and the law of any state merely exists as a function of its power. To paraphrase Oscar Wilde, morality is something we usually apply to those whom we personally dislike.

Hassan ibn Sabbah's motto, however, seems valid only from the Dadaist perspective. Nothing indeed may be "true" in any enduring sense, neither the crumbling pyramids nor the words on this page, which are subject to interpretation. However, using that indeterminacy to justify the conclusion that everything is permitted sounds like one of those desperate blind leaps in the dark that Henry Miller was always exhorting his readers to take. Most of us are far too cautious for that sort of plunge, either blindly or with open eyes. When a writer like Burroughs invites us to enter his sable world, we may do that more with our eyes open than with our hearts receiving.

VII – A Quicksilver Daredevil

Norman Mailer, a writer not given to praising his contemporaries, once remarked that Burroughs was the only writer of our time to have been possessed by genius. "Genius" is a word that writers use too frequently, but the key word here is "possession," and some part of Burroughs' drug use, certainly his use of the hallucinogen *ayahuasca* that he found in Peruvian and Columbian backwater towns in 1952, has to do with the telepathic states he believed drugs could induce and his interest in magic. Herbert Huncke, who initiated Burroughs into the world of drugs in 1944, told me that Burroughs was interested in hypnotism when he met him, another more personal control system bordering on the magical that could be used to affect events.

The essayist Seymour Krim once characterized Burroughs as a "quicksilver daredevil," and I think that phrase captures much of the trickster-craft in Burroughs' imagination. The evolution, for example, of Burroughs' technique from the journalistic naturalism of his first novel, *Junkie*, to the pyrotechnical virtuosity of *Naked Lunch* is remarkable.

Like Joseph Conrad's, Burroughs' major problem as a writer was an emotional blockage, which he overcame only with the shooting of Joan Vollmer. Murder, whether accidental homicide or assassination, is surely a drastic remedy for what is the most common disability faced by writers. The point is that Burroughs would continue to have difficulty releasing his story. He did not have the extraordinary fluency of a Kerouac, who could compose an entire novel like *The Subterraneans* in an athletic seventy-two hour period and never write two novels in the same style. Burroughs was the sort of writer who had to pay for every word.

Some of this payment was epistolary. As Oliver Harris so astutely suggests in his introduction to *The Letters of William S. Burroughs*, much of *Naked Lunch* is anticipated or proposed in the correspondence with Ginsberg. Juxtaposing the letters with fragmentary material and other "routines," he realized his mosaic architecture. But the letters reveal an ongoing struggle. "It is extremely painful," he wrote Ginsberg on October 10, 1955, "trying to weld all this scattered material into some sort of coherent pattern," and he repeats the word "pain" three times in this letter alone.

The use of the "cut-up" followed *Naked Lunch*, which may have creatively exhausted him. Burroughs announced the cut-up technique as a means of new linguistic discovery, a castration of the continuum of meaning that might allow a text some autonomy of its own, some escape from the manipulative control of the writer. The term "cut-up" specifically applies to the scissors Burroughs would use to splice into his text the passages from Rimbaud, Conrad, or T.S. Eliot, passages he would select and arbitrarily integrate into his narrative without explanation or acknowledgment. The term suggests as well the anarchistic humor of a man acting on a stage, a burlesque form for the sake of exposing pretensions. By inserting into his text passages by other writers, Burroughs joined the tradition of accidental art that began with Duchamps and was continued by the Dadaists and then by John Cage and Jackson Pollock.

In one sense the cut-up eliminates a potential for pretentiousness or self-consciousness. It is consistent with what Burroughs told Ginsberg on first meeting him in 1944. Ginsberg, still very much the Columbia undergraduate, asked for a definition of "art." Burroughs' reply was tersely factualist – "Art is a three-letter word."

In another sense the cut-up is his mechanical rejoinder to the warmth of Kerouac's spontaneity. Philosophically, it is his attempt to violate what he called the word lines of Western conditioning and the linearity of old-fashioned art in the way any fundamentally new artistic form affects perception. Psychologically, it was an involvement as well as a way to overcome the paralysis of being unable to continue writing.

The unreadability of the cut-up device dominated and nearly destroyed the value of *The Soft Machine*, *The Ticket That Exploded*, and *Nova Express*, the three novels that fulfilled the *Naked Lunch* tetralogy. To his credit, Burroughs realized the dangers of sacrificing any potential audience, and in his novels of the sixties, particularly in the compelling *The Wild Boys*, he returned to more narrative priorities. But even in *Cities of the Red Night* and the novels that followed, he continued to use the cut-up selectively.

Burroughs was introduced to the cut-up by his friend Brion Gysin. The two men became friends in Paris in 1958, when Burroughs was assembling the material that would be published as *Naked Lunch*. Burroughs told Allen Ginsberg that Gysin's paintings were "the psychic landscape of my own work." The cut-up method, Gysin stressed, treated words in the way a painter treated paint – as a raw material with its own rules.

Gysin's impact on Burroughs was profound, and the calligraphic drawings Burroughs did in Paris in 1958 for the dust jacket of the first Olympia Press edition of *Naked Lunch* reflect the Arabic script and the Japanese calligraphy that Gysin studied. With Gysin in the 1960s, Burroughs worked on photomontage scrapbooks. For several decades, he collaborated with Gysin and a series of other painters, often contributing texts. Robert Sobieszek, who was curator of the show of Burroughs' paintings for the Los Angeles County Museum of Arts in 1996, has aptly characterized Burroughs' own paintings, mostly conceived in the 1980s, as works of "expressive automatism" resulting in a surrealist *terrains vagues* or mindscapes.

In the early 1980s, Burroughs began blasting a double-barreled Rossi shotgun at a can of paint placed in front of a canvas or plywood panels. I saw some of this work at the Tony Shafrazi Gallery in Soho and found it both compelling and disturbing. At first I found it difficult to connect Burroughs' painting experiments with his writing, and I wondered whether the visual had replaced the verbal as a source of inspiration.

Chance, which has been more important to painters than writers, was the connecting link. Burroughs once told me that the final order of the routines that formed *Naked Lunch* was accidental. The progression from chance order as an artistic principle to the random effects produced by a shotgun blast on a panel of paint seems like a natural evolution.

In an essay entitled "Painting & Guns," printed as a miniature book by Hanuman Books in 1994, Burroughs explains the relationship of the visual to the verbal in his work:

> Because it is read sequentially, there is no way to effectively portray simultaneous events in writing. But that's the whole point of painting: multiple points of view can be simultaneously presented. One expands the area of awareness, and one seeks new frontiers in randomness. A shot gun blast produces explosions of color that approach this basic randomness.

Burroughs used a surface of slick paper that enabled the colors to run, and instead of brushes he used his fingers, mushrooms, Pollock's drop device, and a series of other randomizing techniques to increase the accidental or chance aspect of whatever would ensue. His argument, a recapitulation of Cézanne's study of changing light, is that while the artist statically tries to remember a scene or to paint it, everything is changing. So the result is only an abstraction. Burroughs' interest was montage, which was much closer to the facts of perception for Burroughs than any representational art because it locates the reader in the flux of change as it occurs, and as such comes closer to suggesting an illusion of actual process.

VIII – Dream Magic

Burroughs, whose maternal grandfather was a preacher, reminded Jack Kerouac of a "Kansas minister with exotic phenomenal fire." Appropriately enough, perhaps, he spent the last fifteen years of his life in the quiet college town of Lawrence, Kansas, a place once pillaged and burned by the notorious James Gang.

Burroughs died at the age of eighty-three on August 2, 1997. Surprisingly, for a man who had consumed as much alcohol and drugs as he had, he lasted considerably longer than the biblical allotment of threescore and ten years. Laid out in an open cherry-wood coffin in Liberty Hall in Lawrence, he wore a tawny-colored velvet Moroccan vest Brion Gysin had given him, and on its lapels were pinned his honorific florets from French and American academies. Someone read Alfred Lord Tennyson's "Ulysses," one of Burroughs' favorite poems. A professor from the University of Kansas' department of religion spoke about freedom. There was music: Schubert's "Fantasie," Morrocan joujouka, "St. Louis Blues" sung by Bessie Smith. Just before the casket was closed, a pistol and a joint were placed inside. The next day, the body was driven in a white hearse to the Belle Florette Cemetery in St. Louis, where it was buried in the Burroughs family plot, near the monument to his grandfather established by colleagues of the

Burroughs Corporation.

Burroughs remains our ultimate sorcerer of fiction, a space-age Poe inhabiting a landscape of nightmare. Critics already have begun to speculate that the dense thicket of his writing will make Burroughs unreadable in the future, or at best to be skimmed or sampled. Such a facile argument has been leveled at all the modernists, from Pound to Joyce to Faulkner. Hallucination should hardly make easy reading, and Burroughs' audience has always been more select than Kerouac's.

The most surprising thing that I heard when I met Burroughs in 1974 was his insistence on viewing art as a magical form. He argued that in the world of magic, nothing happens unless someone willed it to happen, and there were certain magical formulae to channel and direct the will. What we call "art," he explained in his bone-dry gravelly monotone, was magical in its origins, employed for ritual or ceremonial ends to produce definite effects.

Naked Lunch originally was meant to be about what Burroughs characterized to Ginsberg as an "anti-dream drug," a force used for the sake of control that would destroy the "symbolizing, mythmaking, intuitive, empathizing, telepathic faculty in man." Without the freedom to dream, to conceptualize the new, we become somnambulists in space, no more adept than soulless robots. For Burroughs, the dream faculty lies at the very heart of what artists want. In *Painting & Guns* he points out their purpose is to "dream for other people," presumably even for those who can no longer dream for themselves.

What I admire in Burroughs' work is a spirit of stubborn insubordination that refuses to accept the machine or its robotic agents no matter how efficient they may seem. If Burroughs' obsessively parodic focus on the manipulative games of what he calls the Control Forces frightens us at all, the warning is beneficial, even when it seems bestial.

Call Him Burroughs

Calling partisans of all nations—Cut word lines—Shift linguals—Vibrate tourists—Free doorways—Word falling—Photo falling—Break through in Grey Room.

Nova Express

In fact, biography cannot imitate life; it has to get rid of the chaos and the clutter; it rejects the habitual and extraneous detail of our days; it rearranges its material; it tells a flowing story—something our lives never were.

Leon Edel, *The Age of the Archive*

***

When I was reading letters, notebooks, and journals while researching the development of the Beat writers at Columbia University in the early 1970s, there was very little secondary material to help me form a context. The most obscured life at the time for me was Burroughs'. When I interviewed him in 1974 my purpose was to try to establish an exact chronology.

Now there is a collection of at least a hundred monographs on the Beats including almost a dozen biographical attempts to tell Kerouac's story. Much of what has been published has been disappointing, confounded by myth and presented more for the sake of sensation than truth – sloppy research, undeveloped literary skills, or a myopically narrow focus.

With the case of William Burroughs, who was less in the public eye than his companions, Kerouac and Ginsberg, the standard biography has been Ted Morgan's *Literary Outlaw*, published by Henry Holt in 1988. Morgan had written much acclaimed accounts of the lives of Winston Churchill and F.D.R. so his choice of Burroughs as a subject certainly indicated a radical change in direction. Biographers tend to advocate, but Morgan's was flawed by an overt subjectivity, the way he sometimes paraphrased Burroughs' letters and used Burroughs' fiction as evidence of actual experience instead of literary projection or fantasy.

After Burroughs' death in 1997, the word was that James Grauerholz, his companion, assistant, and literary executor, was working on a biography. Grauerholz did important research into Burroughs' St. Louis childhood, his undergraduate years at Harvard during the Depression, and a subsequent period in Chicago when Burroughs worked as an exterminator and for a private detective agency.

Grauerholz' health suffered a decline and he designated Barry Miles to write the biography, an endeavor for which Miles seems to have been preparing for decades. Miles met Burroughs in 1965 in London, distributed a record album,

Call Me Burroughs in 1966, catalogued his archives in 1972, and collaborated on an early bibliography. The last two are necessary steps for any biographer. In 1992, he published *El Hombre Invisible*, a portrait of Burroughs, and in 2001, *The Beat Hotel*, a book that centered on the run-down little hotel near Notre Dame in Paris where Burroughs lived while preparing the Olympia Press edition of *Naked Lunch* for publication.

Miles' new book is published one hundred years after Burroughs' birth. Even though it is approximately as long as Morgan's, it is more dense, more claustrophobically crowded with detail, more comprehensive. Burroughs lived for another nine years after Morgan's book appeared and he was questioned about lacunae. Also, Miles used an invaluable cache of many recorded interviews made by Morgan now housed at Arizona State University in Tempe.

As a result, Miles has written the best documented account of Burroughs' life we are liable to get. He offers the clearest picture of Burroughs' genealogy and *haut bourgeois* childhood in St. Louis, including the possibility that he may have been fellated by his Welsh nanny or, in a version of *The Turn of the Screw,* prematurely introduced to a view of adult sexuality.

I find it curious that he omits a story that Ted Morgan tells of an early overdose from chloral hydrate at the Los Alamos School in New Mexico, then the most expensive boys' prep school in America, after an unrequited love affair with a fellow student. As a child, and all his life really, Burroughs had trouble sleeping and chloral hydrate is the basic ingredient in barbiturates and sleep medications. Was Morgan mistaken or did Miles just miss it in the scramble to assemble enough details to convince us of his version of Burroughs' life? In the light of Burroughs' decade of psychoanalysis with half a dozen psychiatrists, what such an event might reveal seems significant. If it did not occur, if it was only smoke in the Burroughs legend, why not refute it?

Sometimes, Miles seems so overwhelmed by his own

accumulation of detail as to minimize its significance. He tells us, for example of a shooting accident in Burroughs' Harvard dormitory room with Richard Stern, a classmate, which is presented flatly though it seems quite relevant if the central occasion in Burroughs' life is his shooting at close range of his common-law spouse, Joan Vollmer, in Mexico City on September 6, 1951. Would the Harvard shooting not form a key link in a pattern of irresponsible behavior?

Morgan, incidentally, calls the shooting of Joan "supposedly accidental," implying that he finds Burroughs' stand in the matter suspicious at least. Their union had collapsed and was in a state of taunting, tormented incompatibility. Burroughs was a marksman who practiced shooting obsessively all his life. The most sinister footage in Howard Brookner's documentary film shows Burroughs demonstrating his knives and firearms in his loft on the Bowery. Miles, however, seems to buy Burroughs' view that Joan's death was the result of an insane accident.

I've never been so sure.

Before this tragic event, Burroughs had moved to New York and met Ginsberg and Kerouac. Miles' history of the origins of what Joyce Johnson has called "the libertine circle" around Columbia University and the West End Bar in 1944 is probably the best composite account so far, and he benefits wisely from recent memoirs like *You'll Be Okay* by Edie Parker, Kerouac's first wife.

I admit this is a complicated history that involves three ambitious young writers, a few murders, and psychiatric commitments, but Miles is capable of truncating his narrative injudiciously as when announcing Kerouac left Columbia University because of a leg injury or when trying to explain why he was dismissed from the Navy as "This didn't work out." His relative lack of concern for Kerouac may be only a function of an arch bias Miles inherits from Burroughs himself – the belief that Burroughs' work was superior. Miles also makes a lot of mistakes, minor copyediting errors perhaps, but irritating at times as when he identifies the

D.A. who prosecuted Lucien Carr as Frank Horan instead of Hogan. Hogan had a thirty-year career and was responsible for sending Ginsberg to New York State Psychiatric Hospital in 1949 where he met Carl Solomon.

Miles also never detects what could be a crucial detail anticipating the rivalry between Burroughs and Kerouac which is Kerouac's allegation that he had slept with Joan Vollmer. I saw her name hand listed along with about seventy-five other females in a little black notebook housed at the Berg Collection in New York, all ladies with whom Kerouac privately claimed carnal intimacy. At the same time, Miles does give us a very focused view of Kammerer with his high pitched annoying voice, his obsessively hectoring pursuit of Carr that ended so disastrously when Carr stabbed him with his scout knife on the banks of the Hudson River.

Miles informs us about Burroughs growing cotton and marijuana in Texas, using Rob Johnson's monograph *The Beats in South Texas,* his move outside New Orleans, the rollicking visit by Kerouac and Neal Cassady that is commemorated in *On the Road*, and the subsequent charges for weapons and drug possession which frightened Burroughs into relocating in Mexico City.

Miles' treatment of the years in Mexico, 1949-52, is better than his predecessors' attempts, and he is particularly good at establishing the character of the city, describing Bernabé Jurado, Burroughs' corrupt Mexican attorney, and Lola La Chata, the dowager queen of the heroin trade. To some extent, he relies on the flawed 1995 account by Jorge Garcia-Robles who densely faults Burroughs for not involving himself more profoundly in Mexican culture (Robles' *The Stray Bullet* was recently republished by the University of Minnesota Press). Miles is also drawing on possibly prejudicial research by Grauerholz. However, Miles' version of the central misfortune in Burroughs' life, the William Tell shooting of Joan, is the fullest and probably the most balanced attempt so far to retell a mostly hearsay story based on the vagaries of reconstructed memories.

Burroughs' exculpation was engineered by Jurado, the flamboyant Johnny Cochran of his day, who persuaded Burroughs' pals to testify that Burroughs had dropped a loaded gun on the table and that it consequently misfired. It is a story that might seem more plausible had the bullet penetrated a shoulder or a leg, but it entered near the hairline above her temple. Allen Ginsberg, who had visited Joan with Lucien Carr shortly before the shooting and saw the extent to which she had psychically and physically deteriorated, advanced the argument that the William Tell escapade was an instance of suicide-by-cop, that what she most wanted was an instant out. Burroughs himself, in a letter to Ginsberg written a few years later from Tangier, speculated about the possibility of his own unconscious intent and then added the mystical (and quite unbelievable) explanation that it may have been "as if the brain *drew* the bullet toward it."

Leaving Mexico in a hurry, Burroughs went south to Columbia and Peru, experimenting with a psychedelic vine called *Yage´*. The drug was prepared by local *curanderos* and reputedly enhanced telepathic capacities. It may have helped Burroughs conceive of his basic narrative device, what he called the "routine," which Miles defines as "an extended, wildly exaggerated extrapolation of a simple story" like the Talking Asshole story in *Naked Lunch.* It was a kind of "tall tale" Poe or Mark Twain or Ambrose Bierce knew how to tell though Burroughs could infuse it with a savage intensity that could bring it from vaudeville to an infernal edge. The drug may have also liberated him to imagine the brilliant parody of his caricatures, and freed his imagery with the electric energy that makes *Naked Lunch* so elastic.

The richest section of *Call Me Burroughs* locates its protagonist in Tangier from 1954 to the end of the decade where Burroughs wrote his masterpiece, *Naked Lunch.* Miles has a gift when it comes to describing places like Tangier; of more academic interest, perhaps, is the connection of the people Burroughs meets to later invented characters. The two hundred pages that follow specify with the same relentlessness

Burroughs' activities in London, Paris, New York in the 1960s and 1970s, and his final sixteen years in Lawrence, Kansas when the quality of Burroughs' writing may have lacked the definitive and overwhelming power of *Naked Lunch*. These pages may be of less interest for the average reader.

Anyway, Miles neglects Burroughs' writing in favor of the anecdotal. While this approach makes the biography both lively and tiresome, it should not be relied on for literary analysis. Miles' biography is full of intimate details: a recipe for a hashish confection called *majoun*, Burroughs' love of caviar, and in footnote #5 for Chapter Seven we learn about Burroughs' three most intense orgasms! The reader may wonder whether such information and the multitude of sexual dalliances Miles records are pertinent or even salient, but now, evidently, it has been authorized. The estate-sanctioned biography is almost always partial; the biographer concerned that permission may be revoked if a party line established by an executor is ignored. My mentor in graduate school was Leon Edel who spent twenty years composing his biography of Henry James, but could not uncover James' sexual identity because of estate prohibitions. How can a life be explored if so profound an aspect of any identity is shielded?

Burroughs played his cards out as a pariah figure, an untouchable outcast. He always maintained that his family wealth was overestimated, and Miles points out that the trust fund that helped support him was actually a regular stipend from his parents that lasted until he was fifty. At the same time, Burroughs came from a social class that was quite different from Ginsberg and Kerouac. He went to Harvard, experienced European travel, and he was helped by his parents when in legal difficulties and with buying farmland in Texas. Miles does not tell us (but Ted Morgan does) that the family name was listed in the St. Louis Social Register as his uncle Ivy Lee's was in New York.

Burroughs had thespian talent. He once wrote "every writer of fiction, though he may not adopt the dramatic form, writes in effect for the stage." He could sound like a racist

Texan sheriff or a stupid hillbilly, the leering Hungarian Count or the impervious American. When he played Dr. Benway in Howard Brookner's film, or as a heroin addicted priest in Gus Van Sant's *Drugstore Cowboy* (in a role he seems to have written himself), he demonstrated his dramatic fluency.

Hal Chase, one of the minor figures in the "libertine circle" at Columbia University in 1944, is quoted by Miles as having said to Ted Morgan that "Bill had to posture before the whole world" as if the actor's ability to assume roles was habitual. When Herbert Huncke first met Burroughs he felt "he was heat" and with his hat and raincoat Burroughs often looked like an F.B.I. agent. Miles quotes the Moroccan writer Choukri Mohamed who claimed that anyone who saw him "would get the impression that he was a spy surreptitiously gathering information." Burroughs' penchant for invisibility in Tangier was one of his central poses. It was a function of his fear of the authority he flaunted in his fiction, and his own body language and behavior. It also allowed him the novelist's opportunity to observe closely without being detected.

I interviewed Burroughs, invited him to read at Queens College, audited a creative writing class he taught at C.C.N.Y. in 1974, and met him on various occasions. I realize he had considerable contempt for academics, but every time I was with him I felt the presence of a man assuming an adept disguise. He wasn't a con man, to use hipster language, because he never had a bridge to sell, but he did have images he wished to project and which he wanted believed. At the same time, as Miles contends, Burroughs believed that the "entire fabric of reality was illusory" and consequently may have felt less concern with fame or literary reputation than Ginsberg.

Burroughs is our artist of extremities and such a role requires disguise for the sake of protection (he often seemed aware of potential assault). He understood that since the French Revolution and the advent of new media, the main problem of governance was social control and his fascination with that issue underlies his interest in Mayan civilization or Scientology. His relevance as a writer grows from this awareness and makes him, like Kafka or Orwell, essential for understanding our time.

If biography has any value beyond gossip, its purpose should be to reveal the mask and what it is hiding. In his fiction, Burroughs showed that he was a ventriloquist of many voices. from the genteel to the contemptuous, from the iridescently lyrical to the most vulgar and offensive. What Chase saw as imposture is the acting out of those voices. In the tension between the snarling vitriol of some of Burroughs' invented voices and the banker's look he adopted (like some reincarnated T.S. Eliot, who was also born in St. Louis) we might find the "real" Burroughs.

Through the age of thirty-five, Burroughs suffered from writer's block which Miles notices though he fails to connect it to the unresolved conflicts that handicapped him. *Call Me Burroughs* is full of fascinating new facts –Burroughs learned to fly planes in 1941, for example, hoping to be a war aviator – but in the end, and it is a problem for most biography, the reader feels more burdened by the weighty procession of the factual than enlightened by insight.

So is there room for a different biographical approach? My answer would be what James Laughlin told me thirty years ago when I asked for his help in writing *The Solitary Volcano*, my biography of Ezra Pound: what is needed now is a more interpretative approach, one less devoted to the transient quotidian and one that evaluates the crucial turns in the evolution of any writer.

iv.

"I'm with you in Rockland"

An Interview with Carl Solomon

"Howl," perhaps the best-known poem written by an American since T.S. Eliot's "The Waste Land," is dedicated to Carl Solomon, and partly inspired by some of his more volatile actions. His presence now combines a sweetly naïve idealism, an utter sincerity, an ardor for argument that is redeemed by an instinct for the absurd, and some rare flashes of the kind of quick rage one finds in Blake's portraits of children. The anger was greater when Allen Ginsberg first met Carl Solomon who was being wheeled into a ward at Columbia Psychiatric Institute after an insulin shock treatment – but Carl still had the wit to come out of his coma with a Dostoevskian repartee. Much of Carl's fury in being was dissipated during his eight years of residence at Pilgrim State Hospital on Long Island. The opening line of "Howl," "I saw the best minds of my generation destroyed by madness," evokes Carl's attempts to reach far beyond the incipient apathy of the post-war years for some otherworld of excitement, stimulation, and inspiration. Genius and disease, as Edmund Wilson so aptly suggested in "The Wound and the Bow," are inextricably mixed in the modern artist as each quality illuminates the other. Of this magical reciprocity, Carl Solomon is a representative authority.

Like Kerouac, Ginsberg, and Gary Snyder, Carl Solomon began shipping out in Merchant Marine vessels right after World War II while still a student at the City College of New York. His precocious curiosity led him to search for existentialists and surrealists in Paris, and so he learned about writers like Artaud and Michaux even before they became esoteric. Carl once sent Allen Ginsberg an unsigned telegram that simply stated "VANISHED!" I take it as an index of an irrepressibly anarchic humor and ebullient gaiety, but also as a register of the writer sensing the totalitarian potentials of his age – one can hobo to the road or be kidnapped to the camps. For Carl Solomon epitomizes the Beat notion of the writer as an *outcast* - which is a magnification and a departure from the Lost Generation's idea of the writer in comfortable exile in Montparnasse. In this sense, Carl Solomon exists as one of the key progenitors of the literary underground that has so vitalized our culture with spirit in the past decade.

Called the "Lunatic Saint" by his friends, and feeling entirely obligated to fulfill the implication of that quixotic title, Carl Solomon became the world's intellectual antagonist. His two books, *Mishaps Perhaps* and *More Mishaps*, both published by City Lights, are polemic, impious and impish, controversial, outrageously funny, and a reminder of the sort of suffering our society offers to unconventional minds who would refute its dogmas and violate its taboos. Carl Solomon, who accepted, edited, and prefaced William Burroughs' first book, *Junkie*, was one of the untouchables who motivated the Beat movement; a model of a man who takes risks to define his convictions in an era of easy compliance with authority. He has been somewhat softened by the knocks of time, and now chooses to live quietly in our more rebellious age, but still is, as ever, devoted to words, books, and the lore of the writer.

John Tytell: When did you first travel to Europe?

Carl Solomon: I joined the Merchant Marine in 1945, just before the war with Japan ended. I went to various places, France among them, and I jumped ship in 1947 in France… I stayed there, went to Paris, and learned about Artaud, and Michaux, and Isou.

JT: Isn't it curious that so many writers like Kerouac and Ginsberg were joining the Merchant Marine?

CS: Well, there were movies in those days romanticizing it – "Action in the North Atlantic" with Humphrey Bogart – so that sort of thing was in the air then.

JT: Before going to sea you attended City College?

CS: I started there in 1943, when I was fifteen.

JT: When did you leave City College?

CS: Well, I kept on shipping out intermittently, going to school one term and to the sea the next.

JT: So you were an early dropout?

CS: Yes, although I hadn't dropped out completely. I had neglected my studies really, and I got sort of low grades.

JT: Were there any teachers there that you still remember?

CS: [Henry] Leffert, he was a specialist in Modern Literature – a very sharp, very classy sort of guy who seemed to love [André] Gide.

JT: Was there anyone else?

CS: Then I had Abraham Edel in Philosophy who was very bright.

JT: Was CCNY a very active place politically?

CS: Yes. While I was there I joined the AYD (American Youth for Democracy). This was the Communist front organization of that period when they were anti-axis and for the war. The AYD group was known as the Tom Paine Club. The Communist Party went out of existence then, and they called it the CPA – Communist Political Association – during the Browder period which is now regarded as a revisionist period. Browder felt there would be a collaboration between capitalism and communism, and that the Party should go out of existence. So I joined the CPA which was part of the progressive movement and it was considered the left.

JT: Is this the origin of what is now known as Progressive Labor?

CS: No, no, no. That's Maoist and from the second wave of leftism in the late fifties or early sixties.

JT: Do you remember whether many students were similarly involved?

CS: Yeah. They had a very large membership. As a matter of fact, during those years the Communists dominated the CIO (Congress of Industrial Organizations), and they even elected two members to the New York City Council in those years – Ben Davis and Cacchione in Brooklyn.

JT: Didn't you also attend Brooklyn College at one time?

CS: Well, I broke in with my CP friends that I had made at CCNY, and I moved down to the Village and became interested in avant-garde art and existentialism with a circle of people disillusioned with the left, ex-liberals and progressives I should say. I began to read *The Partisan Review*, and a flock of other little magazines like *Horizon*. I went to Brooklyn

College because I had a friend going there who said that it would be better for my literary interests than CCNY which was geared for engineers and science.

JT: In *Mishaps Perhaps*, you write that you witnessed an Artaud reading in Paris, 1947.

CS: First of all I was looking for existentialists. So I went wandering around San Germain de Pres and came to a gallery with a crowd standing outside. I can't recall the name of the street, but I read an account about it when I returned in *Partisan Review*, how Artaud had been screaming his "Damnation of the Flesh" – I've forgotten the Rue (Was it Rue Jacob?), but to me it's the Rue Impasse or Satan. So I stood outside, and first a young man with black hair descended from upstairs, and he was trembling, and he read what I later found out was Artaud's "Ci-Git" preceded by the "Indian Culture"; then I remembered another man in a turban was screaming. He had been there before the young man. Originally, I had thought the young man was Artaud, but later I learned Artaud was an older man then – he was 51. I remember one line the young man read: "Pappa, Maman et pederastinne" and that tickled Kerouac in later years. The story I gave to him was that the reader was pointing at me but he was really pointing at the crowd.

JT: Did you have any further interest in Artaud?

CS: Oh yes. In 1958 I worked on a ship again since they hadn't ousted me for deserting and I went back to France. This time I got a couple of days off from my job as a dishwasher, and I made the long trip back to Paris just for one day where I bought, in the same neighborhood, Artaud's book on Van Gogh, *The Man Suicided by Society*.

JT: I wanted to ask you about that. In *Mishaps Perhaps* you summarize Artaud's condemnation of all psychiatry, and his argument that those who are in turn condemned by psychiatrists are gifted with a superior lucidity and insight. It occurs to me that such notions are extremely prevalent in radical psychiatry in England and America today with people like R.D. Laing, David Cooper, and Thomas Szasz.

CS: Yes, today. Artaud began to be absorbed in certain areas later on. When I first read Artaud it was still something very esoteric. Later, when the theater of the absurd became prominent, his theatrical ideas at least came through. Anyway, I got *The Man Suicided by Society*, and then moved to West Fourth Street and attended Brooklyn College. At that time I was spending a lot of time in the 42nd Street Library where I found the lettrist magazine, *La Dictature Lettrice*, and read through that. I was twenty years old at the time, and reading Artaud's letters. Then I cooked up a thing with Leni Grubes and Ronnie Gold – who is now one of the heads of the Gay Activists – and we staged a Dadaist demonstration, and threw potato salad at Markfield.

JT: Wallace Markfield?

CS: Yes, he was lecturing on Mallarme.

JT: Isn't there a line in "Howl" about that experience?

CS: Yes. At the time Ronnie and I were discussing the validity of suicide, and I read *Lafcadio's Adventures*[1], you know, the idea of the gratuitous crime, but I backed out of all this. I did steal a sandwich at Brooklyn College and showed it to the policeman, got sent to the psychologist, and then they sent me up to the Columbia Psychiatric Institute. I was in a very negative, very nihilistic mood, things seemed sick to me, and I wanted a lobotomy, or to be suicided. I thought I was a madman.

JT: Was this in any way a reaction to the dullness in the culture you felt at the time?

CS: Yeah, it was a reaction. Just before that my mother and I had moved to Parkchester, which I used to refer to as a Cubist colony because of the way it was arranged – cold, abstract, futuristic, regular houses which are now very common, but

1 A novel by Andre Gide.

that was the first of the large projects. My old neighborhood, Prospect Avenue in South Bronx, had been an ordinary sort of Jewish neighborhood with brownstones.

JT: Was this the Amalgamated project?

CS: No, the Metropolitan Life Insurance Company, and in the beginning they didn't let Negroes in, you know, it was a place where everybody seemed to be a stereotype. And my rebellion against that led to the avant-garde which led to the insulin shock treatment up at Columbia Psychiatric Hospital.

JT: Isn't that where you met Allen Ginsberg in a Dostoevskian encounter with you introducing yourself as Kirilov, and Allen as Myshkin?

CS: Yes, I met Allen after coming down from the insulin ward, just emerging from a coma; comas, no less, to come out of reading and ideas! The story is in my "Afterthoughts of a Shock Patient." When I came out of the hospital, supposedly cured, Allen introduced me to Neal Cassady, and that bunch, and Landesman.[2]

JT: Had you appeared in *Neurotica* before?

CS: No. Before that I wasn't really interested in *Neurotica*, although I had seen it around.

JT: What was Landesman like?

CS: He had an art gallery in St. Louis, a patron of the arts, and as Jack Kerouac characterized him he was a playboy.

JT: John Clellon Holmes has an interesting description of him in *Nothing More to Declare*.

CS: They were close friends.

JT: You met Allen in '49? He had been placed there because of the ride and Little Jack Melody. How many months were you together at that time?

2 Jay Landesman (1914-2011), publisher whose magazine, *Neurotica,* printed work by Beat authors.

CS: Oh, a couple of months, and I got out before he did.

JT: Did you have freedom to meet?

CS: We used to meet on the ward, and write, and read things to one another. I introduced him to works of Artaud and Genet; he read Yeats to me, Melville, and spoke of his friends, Kerouac and Burroughs. But he was highly critical of me. He thought my ideas at that time would lead me to a worse insanity, and perhaps under his suggestion that's what ultimately happened when I went to Pilgrim State.

JT: Well, that is a kind of negative influence.

CS: I suppose it was.

JT: In *More Mishaps*, you write that Allen was taking notes on your adventures while at Columbia Psychiatric, and some of those notes appeared in a different form in "Howl."

CS: He sat there, and I used to come out with very surrealistic aphorisms which he would transcribe.

JT: Can you remember some instances in your life that are reflected, however prismatically, in "Howl"?

CS: The remark about the pubic beards was mine, and the harlequin talk of suicide.

JT: In your books, I thought I detected a sign of hostility as well as admiration towards Ginsberg and his literary friends.

CS: I was angry because of my second sickness. I thought that they had all rejected me because I was madder than they were. I thought that they were neurotics and I was a psychotic, an outsider.

JT: In your books you always tease your readers with differences you had with Ginsberg, such as the way you saw Whitman.

CS: We were continually fighting. I saw Whitman as a political revolutionary, and Allen saw him as a sexual revolutionary. When I first met Allen I called him a "dopey daffodil" because he symbolized to me what poetry was then, referring to Wordsworth, I guess, the idea of poets as sensitive souls rather than Artaud's conception of the poet as brute. But Allen turned out not to be a dopey daffodil at all, but that's the way he looked then, a neat haircut and horn rim glasses. He seemed to me to be like the conventional English major who couldn't stand up to me at all. I thought I was much greater than these types, much more unconventional. I identified with the Beat Generation in much the same way Artaud himself identified with the surrealists: he felt that they were his ultimate enemy.

JT: You mean as a possible close source of betrayal because they couldn't really live up to his ideals?

CS: Yeah. Like when I escaped from Pilgrim State Hospital once I went over to Allen's brother's house, and while he talked to me, his wife called the hospital.

JT: How did you escape?

CS: I just walked off.

JT: What kind of treatment did you receive at Psychiatric Institute? Was it group therapy or individual analysis?

CS: Individual; they had group therapy at Pilgrim State.

JT: What kind of analyst did you have at Columbia Psychiatric – what school was he from?

CS: She – Washington School – Harry Stack Sullivan.

JT: What about Allen's analyst?

CS: I think he was Freudian. We had many fights about our analysts and their virtues. That happens in all hospitals. There was a situation out at Pilgrim State where the gentile patients wanted Jungian analysts, and the Jewish patients wanted Freudians.

JT: In *Mishaps Perhaps* you state that you had been conditioned in illness by classical surrealism.

CS: I meant Artaud's void. Also ideas like the derangement of the senses and things that Ronnie Gold and I used to do. We used to hang out in gay bars then, Mary's and Main Street which were both on 8th Street in the Village, hubs of activity then. They were crowded outside and inside, a real super-decadent atmosphere. Ned Rorem[3] used to go there, he was always at the bar. Ronnie Gold and I used to eat Benzedrine. To me decadence meant absinthe, or green drinks like pernod, or crème de menthe. My idea of decadence was something that made Jack Kerouac write to me when I was at Pilgrim State: "Lautreamont, café noir, sans sucre." I never actually became a junkie or anything like that, and I was probably really afraid of more serious drugs, so I sort of dabbled in safe affectations. Stanley Gould[4] says that I talked my way into all these hospitals, that I gave them the impression of being sick without really being sick.

JT: Do you think you were helped by being in those hospitals?

CS: It was bad as far as my record goes.

JT: I don't mean that, but your general attitudes to life and yourself?

CS: Oh sure. At Pilgrim State, for instance, by urging wholesome things on me, a tame life, the attendant used to treat me like a soldier and say to me "front and center." The psychologists tried to steer me away from the Beat Generation.

JT: Did you learn the lesson of psychiatry as being an adjustment, in fact an acceptance of exactly what you were rebelling against? I would equate that with aging, with abandoning or forgetting youth.

---

3 B. 1923, American composer

4 Lived above Solomon in the Village, and worked together at National Opinion Research

CS: Well, I find myself in that position now.

JT: In *Mishaps Perhaps*, you claimed that your friends in 1949 made you assume the role of a "lunatic saint." Who did you mean specifically?

CS: Oh, Leni and that bunch, like Bob Reisner who was in my class at Brooklyn College, he wrote a book on graffiti. They thought that kind of thing was great. Reisner and I used to do many funny things, like I once pretended to be W.H. Auden at some exhibition, and there I was signing Auden's name.

JT: Somewhere in *Mishaps Perhaps* you mention that you were betrayed by Wilhelm Reich. I couldn't understand what you meant by that.

CS: I have this anger at anybody who has done anything against me or criticized me in any way. So now up in the Bronx I'm just the poor innocent who has returned completely healthy after being driven mad by the captious criticism of all the intellectuals in the Village with their Reich and all the rest of it. And also I go back to the days when I was in high school at James Monroe, where I was into Whitman who seemed to me to be the greatest poet, and all these others were into more Reich. These same people were criticizing me as being overly naïve about sexual matters, but to me they were trying to shock me, while generally mocking me.

JT: How did *Junkie*, Burroughs' first novel, get to you?

CS: My uncle, A.A. Wyn, was the publisher of Ace Books. He gave me a job, and I was trying to make a big impression, and Allen thought it was a great idea to bring out these writers, and if we could make Genet and these others well known to the American public we would be accomplishing something. I don't see what we've accomplished, but we were trying to do that anyway, to change the consciousness. It was largely an educational mission.

JT: And Wyn was interested in this project?

CS: Yes. I don't think he was primarily interested in the commercial end, I think he saw their possibilities as writers.

JT: Did Allen give you the manuscript of *Junkie*?

CS: We got it chapter by chapter from Burroughs in Mexico City. He would send them to Allen who brought them to me at Ace.

JT: That's about Burroughs' earliest writing, although I've read in the correspondence up at Columbia University that he and Kerouac collaborated on a detective book right after World War II.

CS: He sent me another book, *Queer*.

JT: Why didn't that get published?

CS: My uncle and I didn't feel it was up to *Junkie*. That's never been published, but it probably should have been, especially for anybody interested in Burroughs' work. I once made him very angry because when he sent up *Queer*, I suggested that we should change the title to *Fag*, and Burroughs wrote back to Allen saying that he would cut my balls off because he made a distinction between the words, a fag being someone effeminate and a queer is a masculine type of homosexual.

JT: I have a hunch that parts of *Queer* may have found a way into *Naked Lunch*. Did you have any correspondence with Burroughs in later years?

CS: Yes, in Pilgrim State. He once sent me a cryptic note saying I should become a waiter.[5] I didn't know whether he meant that I should wait until I was cured, or whether I should work in restaurants.

5 Burroughs often repeated jokes and ideas, and this is likely the same obtuse joke he made to Allen Ginsberg in late 1959: "Remember I gave you a tip said the Waiter." This was at the beginning of Burroughs' interest in Scientology and he was trying to convert all his friends, while simultaneously alienating them with bizarre in-jokes like this. This "tip" to Solomon was probably Burroughs' way of hinting that he get out of the asylum and into the nearest Scientology processing center.

JT: He was opposed to psychoanalysis. He profoundly distrusts it.

CS: He probably did.

JT: In your preface to *Junkie* you call Burroughs a "curious adventurer."

CS: Because of things like his trip to the Amazon.

JT: As well as mental trips inside the mind. By the way, have you read his more recent work, *The Wild Boys*, for instance?

CS: I glanced at *The Exterminator*; I've been selling it. I'm a little wary of Burroughs now because he's into a kind of general espousal of youth revolt, and it's necessary for me in my present state to keep a very straight, pro-social, even patriotic outlook. During the Vietnam thing I participated in no protests; I voted for Procaccino, and I was on the verge of voting for Nixon, but I ended up voting for McGovern. But at the same time I'm doing crazy things like reading Marx.

JT: In *Mishaps Perhaps* you discuss – not in connection with Burroughs but with Surrealism, - the impulse to make the ugly beautiful which is just the approach I am taking in my own attempts to describe Burroughs' fiction. You also deal with diabolism.

CS: All this is secondary, later than "The Report from the Asylum" which I still consider the clearest statement of my ideas – after that I was just trying to relocate to my legend. That's where the diabolist stuff occurs.

JT: Then you have no chronology in your book because the "Report" is near the end.

CS: Yeah, there aren't any dates. At the time I wrote "Report from the Asylum" I was very careful, and I used to edit closely, but I reached a phase where the whole thing got out of my control, sometimes agreeing to things I disliked out of weariness or confusion. Of course legally, I lost my rights in 1956 when I was committed to Pilgrim State.

JT: Getting back to your work as an editor at Ace, I understand that you were also at one time considering publishing Kerouac.

CS: We had paid him an advance of $500, and I had visions of myself as being his Maxwell Perkins[6] and him being my Wolfe because his first novel resembled Wolfe.

JT: I read a letter you wrote to Kerouac at Columbia University Special Collections in which you said that the Wolfean aspect of *The Town and the City* was a charade that bespoke a repressed surrealism and a repressed homosexuality.

CS: I must have been very erudite in those days.

JT: What happened with the contract because Kerouac never published with Ace Books?

CS: Well, we rejected *On the Road* – he sent us this long scroll. My uncle said it looked like he took it from his trunk.

JT: The teletype roll. Did he get that from Lucien Carr at United Press?

CS: I don't know where he got it, but we were used to these neat manuscripts, and I thought, "Gee, I can't read this."

JT: You didn't accept it as a surrealistic antic, then?

CS: Because at that time I probably wasn't into that. I went through many phases while I was an editor: a Buddhist phase, then when I read this book, *Philosophy of a Lunatic*, ultimately.

JT: Who wrote that?

CS: John Custance. Nobody has ever heard of the book but me. I bought it in the Gotham Book Mart while working for Ace Books. To me it seemed the ultimate mind-blowing thing, going beyond Zen which was a great step toward the elimination of myself. It was an existentialist version of

6 Considered the most famous literary editor, he worked with F. Scott Fitzgerald, Ernest Hemingway, and Thomas Wolfe.

Armageddon, the forces of God against the forces of the devil.

JT: What was Kerouac's attitude to publishers in general?

CS: Bad! He thought of them as skinflints, and he used the term "Broadway Sams" – he meant Jewish liberal intellectuals. He was snide about anybody who worked in offices.

JT: Was there any problem with getting Kerouac to make revisions?

CS: Yes. He got very angry when I wrote him suggestions.

JT: Did Kerouac send you anything after *On the Road*?

CS: Then I flipped and was sent to Pilgrim State. But the house continued to deal with him, and they accepted things, and then later reversed themselves.

JT: Did Kerouac try to interest you in publishing Cassady?

CS: He had mentioned that Neal Cassady wrote, but he wasn't trying to get us to accept anything. That later became *The First Third*.

JT: Did you ever meet Neal Cassady?

CS: Oh yeah. When I came out of Columbia Psychiatric Allen wanted me to throw a New Year's party. So I got a cold water flat on 17th Street and threw a party at which Neal Cassady was one of the star performers. He played one of those sweet potato things that make music, you know, and we were wearing those funny noses with the bebop eyeglasses.

JT: I've heard that Cassady had a magnetic sexual appeal.

CS: Not to me.

JT: What was his appeal, then?

CS: He was always bouncing around – sort of kinetic energy more than anything else.

JT: What about his speech? His rambling monologues?

CS: He did one funny routine at the New Year's party, an Amos and Andy routine.

JT: He was influenced by radio?

CS: He knew a lot about popular culture. He was very American where a lot of us were rather frenchified.

JT: What kind of jobs have you worked in your life? In *Mishaps Perhaps* you have this anecdote about selling ice cream in front o the United Nations.

CS: That was after "Howl" had just come out, and I was considered to have gone mad again. I was working for Eskimo Ace. I've worked on ships as a messman, in the steward's department, as an editor, with books in bookstores, when I was sixteen on a farm in Smyrna, New York, where I shoveled manure and worked a horse drawn plow trying to make even furrows, and earlier, when I was fourteen I bundled the Sunday Times. I also worked for Nugent National Stores in the garment district, and delivered women's wear. When I met Allen we all worked in market research. I was married then, and my wife and I coded for N.O.R.C.[7] John Holmes also worked there.

JT: Let's talk about your own writing. One of the qualities I love in it is your humor which is so often a function of epigram, puns, and wordplay, like calling Poe's "The Raven," "the ravin." Or saying that if you lose contact with the zeitgeist, never fear, you may reach the poltergeist.

CS: The use of puns is not entirely natural to me. That was the Michaux influence.

JT: Can you find ways to sustain that humor in your own life?

CS: I've tried, but it's dropped off. Now my jokes are very bad. I've exhausted my humor, and can't work my brain to that extent because I have to be responsible for my own

7 National Opinion Research Center.

functioning.

JT: Do you feel that you were part of a movement?

CS: As a matter of fact, I hadn't felt that. I had just been through with a movement, and I had an aversion to movements – after all I had just finished with the Communists. I was living on 113th Street, and I knew this guy Don Cook, and he first mentioned the idea of a movement in reference to the Beats, and I was shocked – here I was trapped by something I had been trying to get away from!

The Comedian As Common Denominator

Carl Solomon is known as the dedicatee of "Howl," the most famous long poem written by an American since T.S. Eliot's "The Waste Land." Eliot's mosaic masterpiece was dedicated to Ezra Pound, his friend and collaborator ("*il miglior fabbro*": the greater craftsman). Ginsberg's dedication may be more spiritually motivated than that of Eliot, who was acknowledging the ruthless excisions that Pound proposed to shape the poem. Eliot had written much of his poem in a Swiss sanitarium while recovering from a nervous breakdown; he was perennially unsure of himself and uncertain about the possibility that what he had written was merely therapeutic.

When he submitted his manuscript to Pound, the most confident literary figure of the moment, Pound immediately recognized the poem's universal appeal.

Carl Solomon was less the mentor and more the inspiring friend. The prominent part he plays in the now published annotations to "Howl" suggests how much of it reflects his acts and anecdotes. In 1949 Carl Solomon had been in the New York Psychiatric Institute at Columbia Presbyterian Hospital for two months when he met Allen Ginsberg, who had been remanded there in lieu of facing felony charges stemming from a fracas involving a stolen car in which he was a passenger. Six years earlier, Solomon had begun his studies at City College and Ginsberg his at Columbia University. Going through a Marxist phase, Solomon joined the American Youth for Democracy, a leftist organization known as the Tom Paine Club. His inquisitive nature caused him to begin shipping out on Merchant Marine vessels after the war. In 1947 he jumped ship in France and made his was to Paris, searching for Surrealists and Existentialists (called "excrementalists" by some of the French then). He found a copy of Henry Miller's *Black Spring* in a bookstall on the Seine, and he read it, fascinated by Miller's ebullience – "*C'est pour rire, pas pour lire*," (for laughing, not for reading) he was told by a Frenchman in a bar – but he found more of Miller's books. One day he witnessed an Artaud reading in Saint-Germaine-des-Prés. He became interested in Artaud's book, *Van Gogh: The Man Suicided by Society*, in which Artaud condemned all psychiatry, claiming that most mental patients were gifted with a lucidity that allowed them to see through social shams. When he returned to New York, Solomon was in a very negative, nihilistic state, thinking about suicide and lobotomy. Reading Gide's *Lafcadio's Adventures*, he became intrigued by the idea of gratuitous crime, stole a sandwich from the Brooklyn College cafeteria, where he had transferred, disowning his left-wing entanglements. He admitted his theft to a guard, and was then sent to the Psychiatric Institute.

Almost as soon as Ginsberg arrived at the Psychiatric

Institute, he met Carl Solomon. Ginsberg was nervous, anxious to be assigned to a room, wondering what it would be like to live with a group of men who were supposed to be crazy. The tension of facing criminal indictment had made him unsure of his own grip on reality. When he entered his ward he saw a large man being wheeled in on a stretcher. Emerging from an insulin shock coma, Solomon asked Ginsberg, in a literal tone, who he was. Testing Solomon's sensibility, Ginsberg answered that he was Prince Myshkin, the saintly character in Dostoevsky's *The Idiot*. Solomon retorted that he was Kirilov, the suicidal nihilist in *The Possessed* who is unable to tolerate any signs of ecstasy. The characterization was respectively apt, defining a continuing tension in their friendship. They met freely on the ward for several months, writing imaginary letters to figures like T.S. Eliot and reading aloud to each other. Ginsberg read Yeats and Melville and told Solomon about his friends, Kerouac and Burroughs. Solomon introduced Ginsberg to his favorite French Surrealists, Michaux, Isou, Artaud, and Genet. Ginsberg took notes on Solomon's curious adventures and his aphoristic exclamations.

The two young men had different expectations of the role of the writer. Solomon characterized Ginsberg as a "dopey daffodil" because Ginsberg seemed to represent a Wordsworthian projection of sensitivity rather than Artaud's Surrealist concept of the poet as a brute. In the Psychiatric Institute, Ginsberg seemed entirely conventional, with a neat haircut and horn-rimmed glasses. The two friends fought continually over every intellectual and aesthetic point: Ginsberg, for example, saw Whitman as a sexual revolutionary, and Solomon argued that his political ideas were more important. They also disputed the relative merits of the psychoanalysts: Solomon was being analyzed by a woman, a disciple of Harry Stack Sullivan, and Ginsberg by a Freudian. Ginsberg described the doctors in a letter to Jack Kerouac as "ghouls of mediocrity," claiming that the staff interpreted absurd or eccentric actions as madness. According to novelist John Clellon Holmes, Ginsberg's analyst was soon left confused and completely at a loss, feeling that his patient was saner and surely more honest than he was.

Released from the Psychiatric Institute, Ginsberg began to introduce Solomon to some of his other friends. He persuaded Carl to rent a cold-water flat on 17th Street where they held a New Year's Eve party. Ginsberg introduced Solomon to Jay Landesman, a patron of the arts from St. Louis who edited a magazine called *Neurotica*, one of the earliest post-war publications to anticipate the sexual revolution. Landesman would print both Ginsberg's and Solomon's work. Solomon began contributing book reviews to *The New Leader* and worked as an editor for his uncle, A.A. Wyn, the publisher of Ace Books. In 1952, William S. Burroughs sent installments of the manuscript of *Junkie*, a realistic account of the life of a drug addict, to Ginsberg in New York. Ginsberg showed the material to Solomon, who helped get the book published by Ace.

Solomon later would have two of his own books published by City Lights Press, *Mishaps Perhaps* and *More Mishaps*. The books are comprised of staccato routines, strange anecdotes, and pithy essays, all reflecting Solomon's self-imposed and quixotic role of the world's intellectual antagonist. Called the "lunatic saint" by his friends, Solomon would fulfil their expectations by performing all kinds of weird acts: the perfectly Dadaist gesture of throwing potato salad at novelist Wallace Markfield, who was lecturing on Mallarmé, an act commemorated in "Howl"; pretending to be W.H. Auden at an exhibition and gleefully signing autographs in Auden's name; driving up to Ossining to sit in a car outside Sing Sing prison while the Rosenbergs were executed; selling ice cream in front of the United Nations after leaving his position as an editor at Ace Books. "Every man lives by a set of rules to which he is the only exception," Solomon once wrote. To Ginsberg, Solomon was an instance of the artist as outrage, a man capable of an intuitively quick surrealistic buffoonery that exposed the pretentious stuffiness of the world. Like Ginsberg, Solomon was an outcast artist, an exile within the culture.

Carl Solomon spent the years from 1956 to 1964 as an inmate at Pilgrim State Hospital in Brentwood, Long Island. At that time, it was the largest mental institution in the world, with over 25,000 patients. Ginsberg, whose mother had received a frontal lobotomy at the same hospital, had acknowledged that Carl's commitment triggered the composition of "Howl." Psychiatry, mental institutions, psychic breakdowns may one day be regarded as a key to understanding the artists of our era. And the madness of outrage has not been limited in our time to the Beats: witness the lives of Robert Lowell, John Berryman, Theodore Roethke, Delmore Schwartz, Sylvia Plath – all cases of beleaguered writers unable to bear the realities of the world. Lowell, in writing to John Berryman in March, 1959, seemed to offer a touchstone for the age when he complained of "something curiously twisted and against the grain about the world poets of my generation have to live in."

Carl Solomon, in his "Report from the Asylum," claimed that he had been conditioned in his illness by classical Surrealism. In the years after the First World War, the French Surrealists had used art as a means of protesting the social inequities they opposed, and their style flaunted the bizarre and absurd. As the French photographer Henri Cartier-Bresson has observed, Surrealism was a revolt in *life* as well as *art*, but Surrealist presentation could easily be misinterpreted as madness. This was the case of Antonin Artaud, the French dramatist with whom Solomon identified. Artaud, who ultimately died in the mad house, passionately denounced psychiatry as an agency of social conditioning. Artaud claimed the honest insights of so-called lunatics were intolerable to society. Instead of burning them at the medieval stake as witches, they were encouraged to conform with shock treatments and tranquilizers. For his part, Carl Solomon received seventy-one insulin or electroshock treatments during his years of psychiatric confinement. While in certain phases the comparison to Artaud seems valid, in

Solomon's more vulnerable states there seems to be an even greater affinity with the condition that Franz Kafka created for his victimized characters in *The Castle* and *The Trial*. Solomon was introduced to Kafka as a young man (by Samuel Schoenbaum, now known as a Shakespeare scholar, then a student renting a room from Carl's mother in the Bronx) and identified with what he read. At one moment, Kafka's central figure – who does not even deserve a proper name – can be seen a vehement, enraged, proudly strutting; suddenly, without explanation, he is cowering, pleading, fearing a fly in the room, somehow soiled, degraded, and dehumanized by his terrors. In "Report from the Asylum," Solomon investigates this Kafkian situation as it can be caused by bureaucratically imposed conditions of coma. It is a harrowing inquiry into the "succubus" of shock which would transform anyone's view of the world: "my body, insulin-packed, would become to me an enormous concrete pun with infinite levels of association." The ensuing state shifts from a timeless sense of being everywhere simultaneously to the transcendence of earthly considerations, then panic, amnesia, the Void. The experience seems to approximate our understanding of death, and Solomon becomes a sort of Lazarus returned from the underworld.

Like Franz Kafka, who only published four stories in his lifetime and who ordered his friend Max Brod to burn all his extant writing, Carl Solomon has been a writer without apparent ambitions. He has been one of the marginal underground intellectuals of our moment and his writing has appeared in fugitive magazines like *Neurotica*, *Oink*, and *Exquisite Corpse*. His work exists as a sort of literary graffiti. His particular perspective is that civilization is a joke, that integrity is our supreme fiction, and that truth is blurred and often relative to power. In a piece on Artaud he states that we live in a generation of "charlatanry, propaganda, and corruption, and that there is no room for an honest man on either side of the Iron Curtain." Like Artaud, he argues that most language is merely babble, and that sometimes it would be better to chew bubble gum. While there may be a certain incongruity in such a position, for a writer at least, it does seem related to Samuel Beckett's world as it is defined by its silences and its distrust of language as a means of communication.

Solomon's stance in this no-man's land of muted despair is a bare minimalism and an aggressive comedy. The minimalism is seen in the terse compactness of his expression – a rapid, shorthand definition that often seems elliptical or Surrealist in genealogy. Solomon is not even so much an essayist as he is a miniaturist, microscopically searching for human signs in an alien landscape. What saves his vision from Beckett's bleakness is the quality of his antic humor, a delight in the ordinary even as the banal provokes outrageous gesture when it becomes boring or repetitive. So Solomon the wise becomes the wise-guy, the comedian as common denominator, and his writing becomes animated by the barbs and quips that serve as a protection in an unfriendly world. He sees himself not as the "distinguished poet but the extinguished one"; he says reading is a means of preventing masturbation; he proposes to overthrow the government through farce and violins; he notes that he does not desire to become President, but only absolute dictator with a palace in Kansas built of butter-crunch candy. Like Artaud who knew how to use a hard shell of nonsense to avoid fruitless rational discourse, Solomon's humor often seems an inadequate defense system, the register of a sensibility struggling to cope with vastly superior forces. And when he is very serious, his views often are unorthodox and unsettling. A quarter of a century ago, in an unnervingly understated manner, he pointed to a central domestic debility: "The tendency toward crime among young men of my generation is impossible to surmount." And on a broader social scale he has suggested that there is little difference between those inside and outside mental institutions. Such views may seem eccentric and unfashionable, but on a deeper level they remind us that Carl Solomon has existed as one of the sensitive antennae of our age.

V.
Ginsberg

An Interview with Allen Ginsberg

John Tytell: What was Burroughs' impact on you and Kerouac in the mid-forties?

Allen Ginsberg: Kerouac and I went to see Burroughs in his apartment around Riverside Drive below Columbia, 92nd Street. We were curious. We understood that Burroughs was very intelligent and to us mysterious because he had been to Europe in the thirties, and had married a Hungarian countess, we thought, to get her out of Europe. He showed us pictures he had of Berlin friends in 1936, and told us about people going around and saying, "Won't you have some uppies, my dear?" for cocaine, introducing that whole mythology of old bohemian European use of drugs.

JT: Had you tried drugs before meeting Burroughs?

AG: No.

JT: So that was a crucial introduction?

AG: He didn't immediately introduce drugs at all. It wasn't until about a year later through Huncke and Vicky Arminger who was in that auto crash with me.

JT: The one that Jane Kramer describes?

Carl Solomon: Before you went to P.I.?

AG: There were a lot of Benzedrine inhalers so the first drug was speed which was introduced by Vicky rather than Bill, and then around '45 or '46 through Huncke and Bill Garver and Phil White there was morphine on the scene. So I took morphine at about the same time Bill first did, in the same week. He has described that situation, meeting Huncke, and trying to unload some morphine not knowing really what it was. Bill had a gun he was trying to get rid of, and so he traded it for a box of stolen syrettes of morphine – these were war stocks of morphine that soldiers carried around as part of their first aid. Grass didn't come in until about a year later, in '47.

JT: Was that the first time grass appeared in New York?

AG: Well, for me anyway. Burroughs had had some in the heydays, gaydays of East St. Louis toodleloo.

CS: Ronnie Gold and I used to eat benny inhalers in about '49.

AG: That's what Kerouac used a lot for writing at first, too. And that's what Joan Burroughs took, but she was taking two or three inhalers a day, finally, when we were all living together a little later.

JT: In what other ways did Burroughs influence you?

AG: With books: Kafka, Korzybski's *Science and Sanity*,

Spengler's *Decline of the West*, which he gave Kerouac, Blake, Rimbaud, Yeat's' *A Vision*, Cocteau's *Opium.*

CS: Melville?

AG: No, that was Jack's interest. Especially, a little later, *Pierre*, because of the euphuistic, packed poetical Shakespearian quality of the prose.

JT: And the Gothicism. Were there other books?

AG: Yes. Celine's *Journey to the End of the Night*, Auden, Hart Crane, and Eliot which I borrowed. It was my first introduction to modern literature really, and to also to modern ideas.

JT: Would you say there were any similarities between Eliot and Burroughs?

AG: St. Louis origins, yes. Going to England finally. They also had the same banker look which Bill always had but which he cultivated more later on. Bill actually applied to be in the O.S.S. because he knew Wild Bill Donovan from Harvard, and he was of that elite aristocracy that would have fitted into it, except that he had some early record of having cut off his little finger with a chicken shears to see what it was like.

CS: Wasn't that to get out of the service?

AG: And Bill's hatred of the American secret-police-bureaucracy grows from the fact that they wouldn't have let him in. I mean he *knows* them, that social type and mind.

JT: When were you introduced to gnostic ideas?

AG: The first time I heard the word "gnostic" mentioned was when Kerouac and I went to see Raymond Weaver, at Columbia, who had done the first biography of Melville, *Herman Melville: Mariner and Mystic*, and had discovered the text of *Billy Budd.* Weaver was this great scholar who shared an office with Mark Van Doren, and Jack brought Weaver a novel called *The Sea is my Brother*, his first poetical novel, and Weaver gave him a little list of books to read, like the *Egyptian Gnostics* and either the *Tibetan Book of the Dead* or the *Egyptian Book of the Dead*. I can't remember.

CS: Burroughs' first contact with me was when he read my first article. He said the insights were psychological and not deep psychic.

JT: I felt Burroughs' influence in your last book, *The Fall of America*.

AG: Thematically, yes. But technically, Bunting, saying to condense more, that I had "too many words," getting rid of extra syntactical fat allows more perfume to verbs and nouns.[1]

JT: How come you chose as your Preface to *Fall of America* that selection from Whitman's *Democratic Vistas* on adhesiveness? It seemed so ironic.

AG: Except that it does point to a goal and an ideal and a human potentiality that America was supposed to fulfill because that was the prophecy, the need, and the psychological condition of American democracy, and Whitman named it and particularized it very clearly in that passage. Also it gives credence, historical background, and traditional justification to my own adhesive poems.

CS: I was interested when I read *Fall* mainly in the sex, being a Bronx boy.

JT: In the tender obscenity of poems like "Please Master"?

CS: And "Graffiti."

JT: "Jessore Road" is especially Blakean, its metric, rhyme scheme, and the whole feeling of the poem like a long extended "London."

---

1 Basil Bunting (1900-1985), British poet known for stressing the importance of reading poetry aloud.

AG: The consequence of three years working on Blake songs. It was the first poem I wrote to music with chords, intended to be chanted and sung. I had finished two albums of Blake's *Innocence and Experience*.

JT: I think I saw you singing the poem on television last year with a whole room of people.

AG: Yeah. With Dylan and Happy Traum. I wrote "Jessore Road" to have something really sublime to present Dylan to record. So the performance that you saw on TV was a first performance without any rehearsal because I had finished typing the poem that afternoon, and I had written it the day before.

JT: You have written a number of poems in a very short period of time, haven't you? Didn't you write "Sunflower Sutra" while Kerouac was impatiently standing at your door waiting for you?

AG: Also poems like "A Strange New Cottage in Berkeley" and "Supermarket in California" which incidentally were part of one composition, and later cut.

JT: How were you affected by Kerouac's notion of no revision?

AG: "Sunflower Sutra" is almost completely untouched from the original. It took me a long time to get on to Kerouac's idea of writing without revision. I did it by going to his house where he sat me down with typewriter and said, "Just write a poem!" So I did about the Statue of Liberty, which I never published because it wasn't any good. But I did get the idea of how interesting it could be, the accidents that come up if you commit yourself irrevocably to accepting the traces of your mind during the composition.

JT: What led to your concept of "undifferentiated consciousness"?

AG: Blake.

JT: The experience in 1948?

AG: Which convinced me that it was possible – just like the Cézanne thing, reproducing the *petits sensations* of experience. That's why I became interested in Cézanne after Blake, because when I looked at his painting I got a sudden shock of eternal thrill, that sensation of eternal space being reconstituted – but the experience of Blake was that through poetry you could catalyze in the reader the experience of *Pater Omnipotens Eterna Deus*, an experience of eternal consciousness; but then later on, reading Zen and other philosophy, I would find different nomenclature for it.

JT: In which of your own poems do you think you've come closest to achieving this quality?

AG: I don't know because it seems to happen accidentally, but apparently in "Howl" where it is sufficient to alter people's minds.

JT: What about poems like "Journal Night Thoughts" or "Television was a Baby Crawling Toward that Deathchamber"?

AG: No, that's like a full chaotic consciousness. There is too much excitement and activity in the consciousness, that's amphetamine partly. So it depends on what we mean by "undifferentiated consciousness"… but if we mean empty, *Sunyata*, in which everything comes in quietly, simultaneously, then I don't think I've written anything quiet enough for that – but to get enough excitement to break people's mind systems open, through rhythmic means partly, "Howl" works.

JT: Burroughs was interested in conditioning, wasn't he?

AG: Yeah. Another book that he gave us at that early time was a book by someone named Jacobson called *Progressive Relaxation* which was a sort of Western homemade yoga – just lie down and begin untensing your whole body from the skull to the toes, muscle by muscle and portion by portion, which is similar to the *Satipatthana*, or body-feeling-mind and mind-object meditation of Burmese Buddhists, which is primarily Hinayana Buddhist yoga.

JT: What about word conditioning?

AG: That was covered by Korzybski's *Science and Sanity* immediately when he pointed out that words were not identical to the things that they represent. And the best example of that was when Lucien Carr and I had this big argument as to whether if you carved a walking stick on the moon, was it art or not? Burroughs said, "I never heard of such a stupid question!" In other words, art is whatever you want to define it as it's only a three-letter word. Burroughs' attitude was that we were giving the word an essential identity outside of any use we might make of it, so if we wanted to use the word art to describe the walking stick on the moon, then it was art, and if we didn't want to use the word art, it wasn't. He just said: "It's too starved an argument for my sword," so he cut through arbitrary conceptions like a Zen master. It's like the goose in the bottle *koan*: if you put a full-grown goose inside a bottle with a narrow neck, how do you get the goose out without breaking the bottle, or damaging or bruising the goose? That's one of the first *koans* that you meditate on if you're studying Zen. Another is the *koan* "Does the dog have a Buddha nature?" The Zen master Jo-jo was once asked, and he answered, "Wu," which means no in Chinese. Why did Jo-jo say "Wu"? ... Well, how do you get the goose out?

JT: I don't know. How?

AG: (Claps hands loudly.) It's out! Same way you put it in, with words. It's only a conceptual bottle. So Burroughs resolved the problem of whether a walking stick on the moon was art or not in exactly the same way.

JT: Did Pound reinforce this approach to language?

AG: I hadn't started reading Pound then.

JT: What about when you visited him in '67? Was he talking then?

AG: A little bit, in answer to very specific questions. I have a journal I kept which should appear in the next *City Lights Journal*. I wrote it a long time back, and gave it to Laughlin, and he sent it to Olga Rudge who got upset, and I couldn't at first figure out over what.[2] Laughlin said it was because I had mentioned in the journal how I had smoked a stick of grass at the table on Pound's eighty-first birthday. Then I saw Olga Rudge earlier this year in London, and apparently she objected to my quoting something Pound said to me. He said, "*The Cantos* are a mess, stupidity and ignorance all the way through, and the worst stupidity was stupid, suburban anti-Semitic prejudice."

JT: Why did she object to that? I mean, had Pound said it?

AG: Uh hum. But she maintained that Pound was not anti-Semitic, and it was a misunderstanding to think of him as anti-Semitic in the beginning.

JT: Was Pound's statement an apology?

AG: Well, she didn't want to see it as an apologia, and it wasn't precisely. I think he was just being generous and extraordinarily sociable, and Prospero-like, taking some of the burden.

JT: I know how important Buddhism is in connection with your own work and Kerouac's, but is there any connection to Burroughs'.

AG: There is often an emphasis on open blue space like nirvana or transcendence, of conceptual mind prison... especially in his recent work, the idea of empty space in every direction which is very similar to the Buddhist view of *Sunyata*, oddly enough. "Out of the body experience," or "escape from the frightened, nagging, aging flesh" – that's Burroughs' phrase – is like the Buddhist view of release or *moksha*,

2 James Laughlin (1914-1997), publisher of New Directions. Olga Rudge (1895-1996), concert pianist, mainly known as a long-term companion of Ezra Pound.

liberation from impermanence, from metamorphosis into an unconditioned beginningless and endless suchness, nirvana. But Bill wouldn't go for nirvana as it were; he would see that as a con. But nonetheless what he seems to be after recently, and I think it was implicit all along, is another modality or plane of consciousness where view is unconditioned. The images in all of the books following *Naked Lunch*, like "the blue tide" that comes in on yagé, or the idea of "rub out the words," "all out of the body and into space," as at the end of *The Yagé Letters*, indicate a place that is very similar to the infinite spaciousness of Tibetan Buddhism.

JT: Still, isn't this search, no matter what its end, conducted along a corridor of brutal self-immolation and explosions of pain?

AG: In one view that pain is part of the "apparent thought, feeling, and sensory phenomena," but Burroughs' late theory is that there's a squeeze on the body by a virus coming from Venus to make it as painful a place as possible, purposely contracting everybody into limited space, so Burroughs' remedy is unlimited space.

CS: Did Burroughs and Genet have conversations when they met in Chicago?

AG: Yes, a lot of conversations. I was with them. They loved each other and cared for each other. Bill talked a lot and Genet listened and laughed a lot, and told me Burroughs was very sweet and tender.

CS: We once characterized Burroughs as the American Genet.

AG: Genet told me he had read Burroughs in French, and that he liked his works and his person, and they went around in taxicabs together and marched together in the tear-gas situations.

CS: What happened then? Genet escaped into the sewers or something?

AG: No, the guards said that we had to disperse. So David Dellinger, who was negotiating with the guards, called me up to chant mantras to keep everything quiet which I did for about twenty minutes in this tight situation.[3] Then Dellinger announced that we had been ordered to disperse. We felt we had a legal right to stay. All those who wanted to leave could and the rest would invoke passive resistance, sit on the ground and offer themselves for arrest. Genet being in the country illegally, having come in through the Canadian border, had to cut. So I think Richard Seaver took Genet away, and Burroughs and I stayed… And Genet gave a speech to the Yippies saying that he hoped that some day the skyline of Chicago would be covered with vines, that he felt it was necessary for writers to be with the younger people in body as well as sympathy.

CS: I remember reading that Genet said at the time that he had had much experience eluding the police so it was nothing for him.

JT: I'd like to return to Burroughs' theory of evil. What would you say is its source?

AG: Well, originally it was analyzed by William Lee, the factualist (perhaps representative of a trust of giant insects from another galaxy) in *Naked Lunch*. But since then, in *Nova Express* and *Ticket That Exploded*, and more recently in *Exterminator!* and *The Job* and *Wild Boys*, the agency of the hallucinating Word is a virus from Venus so it's not other galaxies anymore – it's an external, extraterrestrial threat from within our own solar system.

JT: Would you go along with the notion that madness is the norm in Burroughs' fiction?

AG: I would say the norm is metamorphosis. In Burroughs' fiction, madness is the normal behavior of the political world, but it's also a medium that A.J., Benway, and the factualists are

3 Dellinger, a pacifist activist, was one of the "Chicago Seven," incarcerated for inciting a riot at the Democratic Convention.

able to handle and deal with and use as the material for their examination… and sometimes get caught in as is possible for an explorer to get caught in a sticky wicket, or as Burroughs himself feels that he has been caught in certain areas that he could not handle with drugs like psilocybin and LSD, or yagé originally. But madness is *not* his ultimate goal, just the obstacle. This is why Burroughs' geography is so similar to gnostic and Tibetan procedural maps. The wrathful deities are the guardians of the gate to *Sunyata*, blue space… except Burroughs is ascribing all these wrathful deities to a plot by the Control Forces. So his books really are investigations of his consciousness to "trace along the word lines" to the *source* of the control.

JT: So he has a greater conspiratorial sense of history than even you do, I guess?

AG: Mine is a little more mundane like investigations of CIA involvement with dope trafficking in Indochina (which was I think a successful investigation).

JT: What about applying Longfellow's remark on the transcendentalist utopians, that they express the "divine insanity of noble minds"?[4]

AG: I think Burroughs would reject that as sentimental rhetoric because he feels that he is more of a precise scientist investigating regions of consciousness forbidden to common understanding by the Control agencies, and the *danger* of such an investigation is physical pain, madness, "the ovens," but the factualist investigator armed with various antivirus exercises such as rubbing out the word can ultimately resist, though there may be certain aspects which you can't resist… and what you can't resist that most dismays him at present comes in the phrase "At Hiroshima all was lost"… or so he said this year when I went to see him to find out what he was thinking lately. He said that the project was to get out of

4 Henry Wadsworth Longfellow (1807-1882), American poet, most famous for "Paul Revere's Ride."

the body – as the soul or spirit gets out of the body – but the problem with the atom bomb is that its temperature is so high that it's a "killer of souls." So human beings have arrived at a situation where they can be the Killer of Souls. So I said, traditionally, with the gnostics or Buddhists, there is no soul to kill, the void is impervious to the meta-physical heat of the bomb. He answered that Buddhist and Hindu mythology was very amateur compared with the kind of precise investigations that might be conducted now in a highly chemical and technological age. For Burroughs, yoga and Buddhism are primitive methods of achieving detachment; it can now be done more immediately through electronic means.

JT: But less intuitional.

AG: Well, just as he uses the physical table as a place to put his mind to cut up, putting the words on the table rather than inner meditation only – so he sees mechanical aids, like a Yankee inventor, as being a possibility; and also he says we can't turn back, we've already advanced into a highly mechanized, electronic dimension, and that may be the Path. So he puts down the rural commune back-to-nature aspect of what Gary Snyder and myself are doing, saying that it's retrogressive, that we're too deeply plunged into the science-fiction reality of now. For Burroughs the problem is not so much the fact of science or experiment, as it is that it's being *controlled,* that secrets are being kept – like the Army is the only one that has real license to experiment with acid anymore and maybe Scientology is another extension of the CIA network. So his idea is "All secrets out" now.

JT: So resistance becomes openness.

AG: Right, by making use of secret material and turning it against Control Agencies, and by realizing that there are a few simple principles of technology that everyone can understand and master which have been obscured by the authoritarian Controllers. That's why he's been experimenting with the cutting up of sounds and playing them back, in other words feeding back the control images to the Control Center in the hope of setting up anti-image consciousness feedback that will explode in their Control machine.

JT: That's in *The Ticket That Exploded.*

AG: And which he practiced at Chicago when he came into the Convention Hall with his tape recorder with all sorts of riot sounds from Tangiers like shutters slamming and starting spraying all these sounds out on the balcony of the convention, and within an hour the place was in an uproar.

JT: Is the terrifying chaos in Burroughs' fiction purposeful?

AG: I think so. He would maintain that he is making propositions and hypotheses which he examines by means of language and imagination. So chaos – transfiguration is a better word, really – is only the preliminary guardian of the sacred extraterrestrial area of consciousness. The end is not *dereglement de tous les sens* but total silence and calm like a great blue tide flooding the body. And *dereglement de tous les sens* is not even so much a means as it is a by-product of the pursuit through to the other side of phenomena, the disruption of the apparently normal order determined by the CIA and the Control Forces. In fact he feels that they are responsible for the chaotic apparitions, the fear, "the ovens," the images of death. What he is saying over and over, also, is that death is the greatest con, that it has been created by the Controllers to scare everybody, and there's really nothing to fear.

JT: Is he still involved with the Scientologists?

AG: Only in denouncing them. He wrote a long attack on them as a fascist organization in *Rolling Stone*. I went to supper with him and Girodias and heard another terror story about the Scientologists – which is that Girodias published a book attacking Scientology, and they sued him to try and stop the book and they lost the suit, so they organized a letter-writing campaign to the British Home Office complaining that Girodias was a pornographer, and so the Police raided

Girodias and seized 125,000 volumes and drove him out of business in England. So many things like that have happened, so Burroughs has attacked the Scientologists as an extension of the control apparatus that offers people hints of exercises that are useful, but which hangs them up in the middle of the exercise.

JT: How does Burroughs see his own function as a writer relating to this control system?

AG: The virus from Venus (as before a trust of giant insects from another galaxy) or as in other times the CIA, or the economic control monopolists, or the antisex forces, are all resumed in terms of Power Addiction. So Burroughs wants to discover the sources, where the original imposition of brainwash comes from. He sees his job also as an explorer and inventor of how-to books, how to combat brainwash, how to liberate consciousness from the conditions imposed on it by the Control Forces.

JT: So if they can read his books, he is along the way to violating that conditioning by virtue of experiencing Burroughs' own techniques, just as readers who read "The Waste Land" learned a new kind of perception?

AG: Yes. Throughout his books there are all these suggestions on how to observe your own speech and behavior to see who were the people who influenced you and to trace your attitudes, gestures, styles, words, and tones of voice to the original people you were imitating – your father, teachers, lovers, or whoever was leaving an impression on you. Last time I saw him he told me that "whoever leaves an impression on you is a vampire." His statement was so impressive… striking, I mean… curious… that I went home that night and had a dream of William Blake as a vampire because Blake had in a sense invaded my consciousness, left an impression for decades… which was a violation of the Tantric injunction not to cling to any impression. So Burroughs is saying that for his own role he wants to make "himself" obsolete.

“The Greatest Man in San Francisco”

- Jack Kerouac on Peter Orlovsky in *Desolation Angels*

The cover of Peter Orlovsky’s *A Life In Words* presents a corporeal sensation – two serious, staring, bearded men – Allen Ginsberg and Peter Orlovsky – naked and embracing. The photograph, by Richard Avedon, is famous for having been displayed as a poster on lampposts all over San Francisco in the early 1960s, a signal of the gay rights crusade on its cusp. Peter Orlovsky was Allen Ginsberg’s companion for forty years so the inevitable question (which I never asked) was "How does it feel to live with America's most famous poet?"

This rich and valuable collection of diary entries, journal notations, letters, poems, and dreams – gathered from various archives with copious, careful, and helpful editorial commentary by Bill Morgan – answers my unposed query and helps to reveal an unexplained and previously unexplored corner of Beat history.

I first met Peter in the tenement walk-up on the Lower East Side that he shared with Allen Ginsberg in the early 1970s. He was delighted to hear that I taught at Queens College because he had worked as an agricultural laborer on what is now its athletic field. When he was in high school, part of that field had been used as the last working farmland in the borough of Queens. Peter was particularly fond of my wife, Mellon, who photographed him without his shirt while picking a giant stalk of basil on Ginsberg's Cherry Valley farm. He looked like a centaur, or an earthy Mellors in *Lady Chatterley's Lover,* and the photograph appeared on the inside back cover of his book, *Clean Asshole Poems and Smiling Vegetable Songs.* (City Lights, 1978).

Peter was a taciturn, rugged man with a gruff exterior and a submerged, explosive intensity. To Ginsberg, he may have represented an opportunity to merge (as Whitman put it) with the "landscape of the common world." Like Herbert Huncke or Neal Cassady, Peter expressed the Beat notion that writing is not the exclusive province of an aristocratic, university educated elite, that a more vital resource than the library or museum may be the idiom and lessons of the street and ordinary life. The paterfamilias of this view was William Carlos Williams whose suggestion to Ginsberg that an indistinct frontier separated a poet's prose journals from the stuff of poetry became a key ingredient in Beat writing and Orlovsky's where the ideal of spontaneity and the need for emotional release was more of a priority than intellectual calculation and design.

Peter was subject to psychic distress that seemed to have

been a shared familial trait: his parents, as well as each of his four siblings, all spent various periods of time in psychiatric institutions. His father was a Russian immigrant who had difficulty coping with marriage and work, and who left his family early. His mother was deaf and on welfare, her face paralyzed after a botched mastoid operation. In one of his journal entries, Peter remembers a childhood in Wyandanch, Long Island, living in a bungalow near Pilgrim State Hospital (then the largest mental facility on the planet) with a tar roof, a potbelly stove, and an outside pump for water. In another entry he recalls being repeatedly raped in a prison-like foster home. Later, he lived in a converted chicken coop without heat or hot water in Flushing, Queens.

The early journal entries form an anguished record of a shy, often inarticulate youth, suffering from loneliness and the inability to connect with women. The prose reflects his own awkwardness and a groping for grace in language. Sometimes he could blurt linguistic power out of nowhere with a unique fusion of zaniness and existential depth as when he declared, at the age of twenty, to army psychiatrists who were evaluating him, that "an army with guns is an army against love." The remark contains an essential Dadaist truth and a Kafkian poignancy that would earn him a small veteran's disability check for the rest of his life.

He was twenty-two when Ginsberg fell in love with him in San Francisco a few months before the composition of "Howl." Peter immediately realized "Allen will dislike me when I tell him how I don't want to have intercourse with him." Peter was basically heterosexual. Although he describes particularly erotic occasions like a time when Ginsberg fellated him in Tangiers in April of 1957, he was primarily interested in female company and several women (Sheila Williams and Elise Cowan among others) who pursued Allen ended up in bed with him. It was Ginsberg who encouraged Orlovsky to write poems; the relationship was more brotherly or familial than sexual with Ginsberg trying his best to take care of a man who often used drugs promiscuously.

The most tender aspect of *A Life In Words* are the letters Peter regularly sent to his impoverished mother, tender despite or perhaps because of the sexual frankness he displays in some of the letters, and his fundamental concern for his brothers. That concern is at the heart of one of Robert Frank's most endearing films, *Me and My Brother.* Peter worried that Lafcadio and Julius Orlovsky were threatened with lobotomies and institutional care. In a very real sense, Peter was often his brothers' keeper as he tried to live with them in his care, and then felt guilty over his inability to protect them from themselves.

For me the most intriguing reflections in *A Life In Words* are Orlovsky's intimate glimpses of his literary compatriots. Burroughs' *Naked Lunch*, we learn, was originally called "Word" until Kerouac came up with its title while helping to type the manuscript in Tangiers. Despite Burroughs' antipathy for Orlovsky in Tangiers, Peter decides "Bill is a very good man, a bit loony and nervous and strange things come out of his head, but he's harmless and actually very sweet and kind, extremely so." On a subsequent trip to Peter's own family in Northport, Long Island, a town where coincidentally Kerouac was living with his mother, Peter notices Kerouac's notebooks stacked high in a pile of thirty, and also concludes that Kerouac is a Zen lunatic "drunker than a dog's tail." Unfortunately, there are few such glimpses and more record of conflict or resentment of figures like Gregory Corso who denigrated Peter's poetry and was often condescending.

In general Orlovsky's journal entries seem fragmented, notations more than sustained inquiries, partial accounts that focus on his distress without creating for the reader the narrative coherence of a life. Perhaps this is asking too much of an occasional diary that assembles four decades of reflection. Sometimes, the writing seems forced or labored, a feeling I had when reading Neal Cassady's *The First Third.* While it is true that what brought the Beats together in the first place was their mutual interest in writing, they weren't all able to do it on the same level of accomplishment.

Large parts of the journals are devoted to Peter's *dharma* wandering through Mexico, Europe, Morocco, the Middle East and India. These sections lean towards flatness, lacking the dimensions of place and the anthropological density and detail of Kerouac in *Windblown World* or Ginsberg in his journals. While there are nuggets of discovery observed with innocent wonder – the old men in burlap in Tangiers, the white veiled women wrapped in swathes of white cotton, a long line of naked *sadhus* in Hardwar waiting to bathe in the Ganges – such moments are rare.

The Buddhists may argue that all comparisons are invidious, but to accept such a proposition is to deny the validity of any criticism. Part of the problem for me with reading *A Life In Words* is that Peter was essentially not a wordsmith. There are a few flares of dynamic expression in some of the poems and poem fragments that Morgan includes, especially one composed entirely of thirty-six unanswered questions written in June of 1959. The final question in the poem, "are you on earth to talk or walk?" seems central to Orlovsky's situation, and at one point in the collection when he is in Lebanon he speculates on the possibility of walking from Beirut to India. It is a guru path for sure and Peter was on it though he may have stumbled frequently along the way.

There were trips and falls as well. The last part of *A Life In Words* feels a bit like scattering leaves and illustrates the despondencies and desperation of addiction. One consequence for Peter was increasing silence, the inability to find the words. The last time I saw Peter was in a dim, grim room right near the end of the twentieth century in a halfway house for recovering addicts on Broadway and 100th Street, a block from where I spent my childhood. Mellon and I walked with Peter to the Soldiers and Sailor's Monument, a few blocks away on Riverside Drive, so he could smoke a cigarette. He seemed like a ghostly shell of a man, absent, resigned, wry and sorrowful.

There is a particularly touching photograph at the end of the book, supposedly the last one taken by Ginsberg a day before his death, of Peter standing with his hand on Robert Frank's shoulder. Mellon and Robert Frank always wanted to drive up to St. Johnsbury, Vermont where Peter spent his final years, but we never were able to organize that trip. I regret that missed adventure because Peter was always able to offer genuine glimmers of poetry along his way.

Requiem for Ginsberg

Unscrew the locks from the doors!
Unscrew the doors themselves from their jambs!
- Walt Whitman, "Song of Myself"

I - The Final Year

Allen Ginsberg opened the doors of poetry, of perception, of a freer life, with so cleansing a candor in such a polluted time. He was the greatest poet and teacher I've known.

I met him at his farm in Cherry Valley almost half a century ago. Full of scholarly curiosities and the impertinent questions of biography, I was working on *Naked Angels* –

Allen's benevolent advice was to call it *Naked Humans*. Allen was always a willing historian, concerned with accuracy and emotional truth. I remember spending hours in fields with him, talking about Burroughs and Kerouac while picking vegetables.

Ginsberg had the best understanding of Burroughs' and Kerouac's work. For Kerouac, he wrote the introduction to *Visions of Cody* and to *Pomes All Sizes*. When I did the interview, which was subsequently published in *Partisan Review*, half of it constituted a critical discussion of Burroughs' work. I still haven't read anything on Burroughs that surpasses its perception.

I would see him intermittently over the years, sometimes spontaneously – the key thrown from the window on 12th Street – but more often at the Beat gatherings that have occurred with frequency of late. At the twenty-fifth anniversary reading of "Howl" at Columbia University, it took Allen twenty-seven minutes to read a poem that I had heard him read at the Judson Church in twenty-two minutes. When I asked him about the discrepancy, he explained that the breath of those long strophes was now more difficult to manage. It was my first intimation of his mortality.

The Judson Church reading occurred in the early 1960s. Ginsberg had invited the Russian delegation to the UN, who walked out in formation, twenty men in gray suits with close-cropped hair, offended by the first part of the poem. No wonder Allen was ejected from Czechoslovakia in 1965 after students crowned him King of May. The Communist puppet Czech government (like the Cubans later) claimed Ginsberg had been deported for seducing youth, but the actual reason was sedition – ie talking freely – the kind of talk no totalitarian system can tolerate.

Everyone knew that Allen was frail, but we were amazed at how well he could recover. At the Kerouac Conference that NYU organized in 1995, Allen had a pulmonary embolism, and his physician ordered rest. Instead, Allen spoke to several hundred people about Kerouac, as intent on spreading his word as he had been when I first interviewed him in Cherry Valley. Then he left for Europe to give a reading.

That sort of enthusiasm – the best word to characterize him, really – was the igniting spirit of his poetry. Early in 1996, I saw Kazuo Ohno, a ninety year old *butoh* dancer at the Japan Society. It was one of the most astonishing dance performances I've ever seen, one that defied all the expectations associated with aging and indeed death itself. After the ovation, as the audience was filing out of the auditorium, Allen remained in his seat, furiously writing in a little notebook. He continued until long after everyone had left, his diamond intensity as concentrated as Ohno's.

In the fall of 1996, at Gary Snyder's reading on Union Square, Allen's skin looked extremely sallow – an orange hue – and when he kissed me I thought it would be the final time.

On February 16th, 1997, Mellon went to a morning teaching by Gelek Rinpoche, Allen's Buddhist guide, at the Jewel Heart Center in the American Thread building and sat next to Allen. When she returned home, she told me Allen looked like rigor mortis. This was unusual, because Allen – who questioned reincarnation – was sometimes rebellious with the Buddhists, and capable of asking impossible questions.

I saw him the following night, on February 17th, at the Carnegie Hall benefit for the Tibetans, and he was just sublime. Backed by Michael Stipe and Billy Corgan,[1] he sang "Put Down Your Cigarette Rag" and the "Ballad of the Skeletons." That mordant eighteenth century homiletic encapsulated his lifelong condemnation of what he called Moloch in "Howl" or what Burroughs called the "Control Forces" – corporate oligarchy, lobbyists, and Big Government.

For me it was the essence of what I had always seen in Allen, what he described as bhakti yoga, the pure delight of salvation by singing. The result was transcendental – which is why he was our Whitman – rhapsodic and ecstatic.

---

1 Michael Stipe is the lead singer of the band REM, and Billy Corgan is from Smashing Pumpkins.

II – The Final O

Early in the morning of April 4th, 1997, Mellon's birthday, I had a peculiar dream. I was eating lunch with Carl Solomon in a greasy-spoon diner, the kind Carl favored, located on the second floor of a building near Washington Square. Carl finished his tomato soup, coughed loudly, and excused himself to go to the men's room.

Turning my head, I noticed Allen Ginsberg in a worn gray suit near the cashier's register, framed in the doorway and exiting. I rose to greet him and followed him through the door onto a stairway landing. Lots of people were moving up and down the dark, narrow stairway. I saw Allen moving up, rounding the corner in a spot of light at the top of the landing above. He did not hear when I called to him, but continued his ascent.

I returned to my table, and the waiter approached to inform me in a matter-of-fact manner that my table companion – meaning Carl – had dropped dead while in the men's room.

I woke from the dream to relate it to Mellon, realizing dimly that this was hardly the way to begin a birthday, but the load seemed too heavy not to be shared. Relating the dream was momentarily confusing because Carl had actually died in 1994, a few years earlier.

Forty-five minutes later, doing yoga, we heard announced on National Public Radio that Allen had terminal liver cancer. What we did not know was that he had been released by Beth Israel Hospital a few days earlier, conveyed in a wheelchair by his assistant Bob Rosenthal three blocks through the streets to his new loft on 14th Street.

On April 4th, Allen took a bad turn – possibly he suffered a stroke. Many friends were with him, including Peter Orlovsky, his lover for over three decades, and Gregory Corso, Patti Smith, and Larry Rivers from the loft above, wandering about in pink, white, and blue-striped pajamas.

Ginsberg's friend Rosebud Pettet described his final hours

in the tribute at St. Mark's Church. Allen, in a Jewel Heart T-shirt, lay in a narrow bed, under a photograph of Whitman. His breathing was extremely labored; he was really gulping for air, although there were tubes from his nostrils attached to a portable oxygen tank.

Incense mingled with the scent of flowers. A group of Tibetan monks led by Gelek Rinpoche, his instructor in dying, were chanting and praying. At two-fifteen on the morning of April 5th, illuminated by a single low light, Allen suffered a convulsion. Peter Orlovsky kissed his head, saying, "Goodbye, darling."

Rosebud Pettet noticed a tremor, and then, as she described it,

> slowly, impossibly, he began to raise his head. He weakly rose until he was sitting almost upright, and his left arm lifted and extended. Then his eyes opened very slowly and wide. The pupils were wildly dilated. I thought I saw a look of confusion or bewilderment. His head began to turn very slowly and his eyes seemed to glance around him, gazing on each of us in turn. His eyes were so deep, so dark, but Bob Rosenthal said that they were empty of sight. His mouth opened, and we all heard as he seemed to struggle to say something, but only a low soft sound, a weak "aaah" came from him. Then his eyes began to close and he sank back onto the pillow. He continued, then, to struggle through a few more gasping breaths, and his mouth fell open into an O.

III – The Candor Man

Unlike most people who begin so brilliantly, Ginsberg never burned himself out, but continued to create remarkable poetry. After his death, in what amounted to a last-page editorial in the *New York Times Book Review*, its editor, Charles McGrath, asserted that Ginsberg had failed to match the genius of "Howl" and "Kaddish." This has been the perennial establishment view of Ginsberg, a cliché of criticism that has been routinely applied to great poets from Wordsworth to Whitman. The attitude is condescendingly wrong, as silly as claiming Whitman's only great poem was "Song of Myself." Ginsberg's imagination as a poet was always at the borders and beyond, inventing the new. If you don't share this belief, consult Helen Vendler, or read the tribute she contributed to *The New Yorker* of November 6th, 1996, six months before his death.

Most of the critics haven't quite understood Ginsberg's humor – to call it Surrealism is a misunderstanding – and they have had a continuing problem with what John Hollander once criticized as Allen's decorum. The feeble argument that Ginsberg is more imposing as a cultural force than as a poet only marginalizes poetry more than need be. "Literature is news that stays news," Ezra Pound once declared, and beside a certain element of bombast in Pound's pronouncements on poetry is often a brilliant truth.

"I would call that man poet," Henry Miller wrote, "who is capable of profoundly altering the world." Ginsberg changed the world of poetry with the overwhelming excess of "Howl." He put his "queer shoulder to the wheel," as he promised in his poem, "America," to do his best to better the world. Ginsberg had less fear – of convention or the state – than any other man I've known. Allen believed that things could change, that no authority was absolute, and in the service of such notions he was a main organizer of the protests against the Vietnam War and of what is called the "counterculture." This was a persistent commitment, so, for example, on July 14th, 1978, he sat meditating with Peter Orlovsky and three young women on the railroad tracks in Rocky Flats, Colorado, impeding the progress of a train transporting fissionable materials.

Our principal spokesman for candor and spontaneity in an age of secrecy and denial, he offered his remarks on censorship or psychedelics to congressional committees or *People* magazine. But Allen's ambition was not only political; because he believed in poetry, he supported a number of poets, accommodating some of them and their families at Cherry Valley. With his "palsied lip," as he put it in a poem on teaching at Brooklyn College, he was nevertheless the most passionate reader of poetry since Dylan Thomas, a fact some academicians still suspect as much as his capacity to fill a big room almost anywhere in this country with those eager to hear him. It is no wonder that no other poet in our time has been so memorialized, in Brooklyn, Berlin, Barcelona, and Calcutta, in San Francisco and LA, in Central Park and City Island, in the Cathedral of St. John the Divine and in Times Square.

Ginsberg was always able to Make It New, as Pound had urged, and to make his poetry relevant to our general spiritual needs. Both Pound and Ginsberg had the rare capacity to be both avant-garde and Old Master simultaneously. I find it so charming that in Venice in 1965 Ginsberg chose to play Bob Dylan and the Beatles for Pound, then seventy-nine and locked in his decade of silence, because he felt the older poet should hear the new sounds.

Ginsberg jammed with Dylan and with John Lennon, the way Kerouac had with Lester Young, because a great poet, as Pound had taught, first of all was a musician.

"When the mode of the music changes," Allen once told me, loosely paraphrasing Pythagoras, "the walls of the city shake." And his life was spent shaking those walls with his own music, beginning with the Blake that he loved, put to song, and recorded. Many musicians – from Lou Reed to Patti Smith – sang or spoke at the St. Mark's Church memorial, which lasted for five hours with a line around the block despite the pouring rain.

Our Zeitgeist poet in a particularly dark time, Allen Ginsberg was the main singer of our generation. The songs he sang for us will continue to be sung as long as we have the voice and the heart to sing them.

www.ingramcontent.com/pod-product-compliance
Lightning Source LLC
Chambersburg PA
CBHW070033120726
47909CB00003B/1145

9780956952592